WELLS FARGO
THE LEGEND

DALE ROBERTSON

WELLS FARGO THE LEGEND

Etchings by Roy Purcell

CELESTIAL ARTS
Millbrae, California

Our grateful thanks to the people of Wells Fargo Bank
for their help in checking the manuscript for accuracy.
In particular, we want to thank Merrilee Dowty and
Elaine Gilleran of the Wells Fargo Bank History Room.
However, any errors that remain are the responsibility
of the authors.

Dale Robertson
Roy Purcell

Copyright © 1975 by Dale Robertson and Roy Purcell

Celestial Arts
231 Adrian Road
Millbrae, California 94030

First Printing, November 1975

1 2 3 4 5 6 7 8 9 10 -- 80 79 78 77 76 75

Made in the United States of America

Library of Congress Cataloging in Publication Data

Robertson, Dale, 1923-
      Wells Fargo, the legend.
      1. Wells, Fargo and Company—History.   2. The
West—History.
I. Title.
HE5903.W5R62   388.3'2'06578   75-9070
ISBN 0-89087-177-9
ISBN 0-89087-064-0 pbk.

CONTENTS

CHAPTER I

PRELUDE TO DESTINY!

The first tiny fingers of sunlight were probing at the eastern hills as the foreman strode through the work camp. Here and there sleep-logged men were shedding their blankets; shivering, their teeth achatter from the wintry gusts, they stomped the frozen ground in an effort to warm their feet as they dressed in the cold, gray dawn.

Spotting Pete Wimmer on the steps of the crude building that served as headquarters and cookshack, the foreman waved authoritatively, beckoning him to his side. As the man crossed the campsite the foreman nodded with approval. Wimmer, an excellent wheelright, had certainly filled the bill as assistant during the construction of the sawmill. A hard worker, he had earned his men's respect and they had shown it by cooperation and teamwork. But a lot of credit was due Wimmer's wife for the harmony in the camp. She had left the comforts and safety of the fort and trudged forty rough miles at her man's side to serve as main cook and nurse for the work camp. And there was no doubt in the foreman's mind that her tasty hot biscuits and apple cobblers were mainly responsible for keeping down the grumbling and fighting that usually went on in a crew of this size!

1

As Wimmer reached his superior's side most of the workmen were dressed and streaming past, heading for the warmth of the cookshack and the strong hot coffee waiting there. The younger man listened carefully as the foreman laid out the day's work load; Azariah Smith and his partner, Bill Johnson, were to keep on felling trees, Alec Stephens and cantankerous Jim Barger hewing and trimming the rough lumber, the Virginia Mormon, Henry Bigler, was to drill at the head of the race while Charley Bennett and Will Scott were scheduled to work at the bench. The rest of the crew, mainly Indians, were to continue the digging and to take care of any camp chores that Wimmer deemed necessary. When the foreman had finished speaking Pete Wimmer nodded and turned away to relay his instructions to the men, most of whom were now seated at the long, rough-slabbed tables of the cookshack "sopping" hot biscuits and gravy.

As Wimmer entered the cookshack, the foreman stared at the ominous gray skies scudding overhead. His brow furrowed. No one knew better than he what another vicious snowstorm would do to the carefully laid timetable of the work camp. Too well he remembered the previous winter when George Donner's party had become marooned in the treacherous mountain passes a hard day's ride to the north and east. Out of food and starving, the survivors had been forced to eat the flesh of their own dead in order to survive! Now the stigma of the Donner party hung like a malodorous shadow across this land, serving as a painful and constant reminder of its cruel winters and other dangers.

He turned and walked toward the tailrace for his morning inspection, his mind churning with its worries as he talked to himself. Well, at least the sawmill should be finished in another month to six weeks. The main thing left to do is to deepen the tailrace that channels the stream back to the river bed after the water has served to power the big wheel. As he walked his keen eyes spotted several places where Pete's men needed to deepen the course.

Suddenly he halted in his tracks, his eyes narrowed. Streamers of sunlight were shimmering from the bottom of the tailrace, reflected from a multitude of tiny golden flakes! Deeply curious, he bent over to study them more carefully. His fingers probed at the icy, numbing waters, pawing about until they had trapped a few of the tiny metal bits. Holding them in a big, work-calloused hand he studied them closely. Could this be . . . no, that was ridiculous. This couldn't be gold. Or could it? His mind delved into the past, recalling what little he knew about such things. Time and again gold-strikes had been reported, one even as far back as '42 when some fellow had claimed he found gold in Cahuenga Pass, just outside of the sleepy little pueblo of Los Angeles. But nothing had come of that, or of any of the others either for that matter. And for a fellow to even hint he'd found a bonanza, well, it was like admitting you were some kind of jackass. No, this couldn't be . . . Suddenly, on an impulse, he beckoned a nearby worker to his side and sent the man on an errand.

Fifteen minutes later the foreman had scooped several handfuls of sand and gravel from the tailrace into the pan the workman had brought from Mrs. Wimmer's kitchen. Gently he swirled the water in the pan as he tilted it, gradually washing out the sand and gravel. As he worked at his task, tongue playing at the corner of his mouth, he was a study in concentration. At last he was finished. He stood rooted in his tracks. At the bottom of the pan was enough of the golden metal flakes to cover a ten cent piece! His hands trembling slightly, he refilled the pan and repeated the "panning" process. This time there was even more of the shiny metal in the pan. Slowly, he walked back to the camp and his quarters, his mind awhirl. Closing his door he sat down in a rough chair and pursued his thoughts. Gingerly he opened his Barlow and probed at one of the largest flakes. He cut at it, noting that it was hard and retained it's shape, despite the sharpness of the knife. He placed the tiny kernel between his teeth and bit down as hard as he could with no results. He stared at the yellow metal flakes. There was no doubt whatsoever in his mind that he had struck a bonanza. Excitedly he began to consider his next move. What would a goldstrike mean to him and the camp? In his mind's eye he pictured hordes of greedy goldseekers that would swarm down upon the camp as soon as the news leaked out. How should he handle it? Tell everyone and let the workers have a chance to stake their claims before the outsiders could overrun the campsite? If he did, was there any way that he could get his crew to stay and finish the sawmill before they went prospecting? All the rest of the day he stayed locked in his quarters, seeking answers to his newly discovered problems.

In the end, his basic honesty won out. After the crews had finished their meal that evening he called them together in the cookshack. As he lolled against a wall waiting for them to assemble there was an air of suspense. The workers eyed him closely, wondering what could possibly be so important enough for him to call them together? As they waited for the others to arrive some of the men lit their pipes. Soon the aroma of pipe tobacco was mingling with the stench of unwashed bodies, and the smell of coal oil, dried fruit, creosote, vegetables and other goods stored in the pantry of the cookshack.

At last the crew was assembled; those too late to find chairs squatted around the walls of the rough building or stood at the rear of the room next to the huge fireplace. When the coughing and scuffing of feet died down the foreman stepped forward, raising his hand for their attention. He reached in his pocket and removed a small tobacco sack. All eyes were upon him as he slowly and ceremoniously poured the contents of the pouch into the palm of his left hand and tilted it in the rays of the nearest lantern for them to see.

He spoke, his words slow and careful, "Men, I've called you here to talk about something that could change all of our lives." He paused studying their reactions. The room was deathly still as he continued, "I think I've discovered gold!"

For a moment they digested his words, trying to see if he was serious or making some sort of joke. Then suddenly the silence was shattered by laughter, much to the foreman's discomfort.

From the dim shadows at the rear of the room one of the men cried out, his voice mincing and in jest, "Yeah, and I'm the King of England! How-de-doo, you all!"

Gales of laughter continued as the others reacted to the funster's words.

Several of the older men exchanged glances, shaking their heads gravely. As each of them knew, there wasn't a man in the place that hadn't thought he'd found "color" at some time of his life. But always their so-called strikes had proven to be nothing more than pyrite, otherwise known as "fool's gold."

The foreman had seen enough. Obviously he had made a mistake in broaching the subject. Now he sought to repair the damage and retain as much face as possible. "I know, I know what most of you are thinking. You figger this is nothing but "fool's gold." Well, maybe it is, but I've seen "fool's gold" and this, well, this is different, somehow. Of course, since so many of *you* seem to be experts on the subject maybe you can tell me how to test it so that I'll know if it's gold or not?"

The laughter died away and once again silence fell upon the room as men stared from their foreman to each other. A few voices called out hesitantly from around the room as they strove to recall what little they knew about the matter.

"Well, fer one thing, it's er . . . well, gold's heavy as all getout!"

"Yeah, and I hear tell ye kin beat it and maul it with a hammer but that don't really hurt it none."

"Yep, I knowed a feller who beat the hell outta a goldpiece but even though he finally got it real thin it wuz still hard and you could tell it wuz *real gold!*"

Another voice or so started to sound off but died away as their owners realized they had nothing concrete to add.

Suddenly a small hand waved timidly from the rear of the room. Pete Wimmer's wife had looked on and listened as the discussion progressed, fully aware that this was man's business. But now, seeing that no truly helpful suggestions had come from the meeting and desiring to help in any way possible, she steeled herself to speak. Instinctively the hubbub died down, attesting to the respect the assembly had for her fried apple pies and other culinary achievements.

The foreman nodded encouragement, "Yes, Mrs. Wimmer?"

"Well sir, I don't mean to butt in, but I think that if anything we've got in camp would really test the metal it would be lye."

For a brief moment her listeners evaluated her words, then heads nodded here and there, agreeing with her logic.

The foreman eyed his crew, nodding. "Mrs. Wimmer, that's the best advice I've heard all night." He paused, weighing his audience. Obviously they were skeptical about his discovery and no amount of talk on his part would change their minds. Just as well, he told himself. The last thing he needed was for them to catch "gold fever" and go off staking claims, leaving the sawmill unfinished and doomed to failure. He signaled again to still the undercurrent of noise and continued, "Well, if I still think I've found gold in the morning I might try testing it with lye. In the meantime we'd better get to bed so that we can fall out at daybreak. That's all." As he turned away the dismissed workers straggled out the doors, discussing the events of the meeting.

The foreman caught the eye of one of the men and walked with him a few yards away. He studied the man for a moment, then spoke, "Bigler, I am probably wrong about what I found but it won't hurt to check it out. Now I want you to go down and shut the head gate and make it tight. Then we'll see what the morning will bring."

As Bigler nodded and moved to comply, the foreman

strode purposefully back to his room. Locking the door and pulling a blanket across his sole window he busied himself stoking the fire. Fifteen minutes later he was pouring the contents of the small tobacco sack into a pan of water boiling on his campstove. Then, slowly and cautiously, he poured a can of lye into the water, stirring as he did so. Tossing the empty can into a trash box, he settled down on the rickety bed to wait.

Roughly an hour later he was still checking the boiling pot from time to time. Using a small long-handled ladle he dipped into the water and fished out a few of the shiny flakes. Holding them close to the dim coal oil lamp he eyed them carefully, looking for any sign of attrition. The blood was pounding in his temples as he finished his scrutiny. *There was no visible evidence that the lye had harmed the metal in any way!* He nodded his head. Now he was surer than ever that he was right. *He had discovered gold!* Restlessly he settled into his blankets. Tossing and turning, his mind rolling with thoughts of what the future would bring, he lay for hours before sleep finally came.

At first light he was waiting at the tailrace. He nodded with satisfaction as he noted Bigler had carried out his orders. As the sun inched over the horizon and lit the area he chuckled to himself. Here, there, everywhere in the rushing water he could see tiny golden flakes. And there was much more than he had found the previous morning! Quickly he started collecting them. A few minutes later he had gathered roughly about three ounces of the yellow metal, including one nugget about the size of a small kernel of grain. Satisfied, he headed back to the camp, meeting some of his men who were headed to the tailrace to start their day's work. He waved good morning, saying nothing about his latest findings and continued to his cabin. Once again he shut himself in his cabin and began to pace back and forth, pondering his next move.

During the day a cold wintry rain began to fall, from time to time turning to sleet as the temperature lowered. Back and forth the foreman strode in his one-room quarters, oblivious to the rain, sleet, and everything but the small pouch lying on a nearby table.

It was almost dark when he left his quarters to saddle his horse and lead it from the muddy corral. With no word to anyone, unmindful of the rain pelting down, he rode off into the darkness. All night long he rode, numbed by the chilling rain but burning with the fever deep within him!

The dog-eared diary of Capt. John Augustus Sutter bears one brief entry for the date of Friday, January 28, 1848; "Mr. Marshall arrived from the mountains on very important business."

Later the servants were to tell of mysterious doings, secretive experiments and other weird goings-on during the few hours the foreman stayed at the fort. And then, despite the protests of Capt. Sutter, the weary foreman crawled back into his saddle and rode the forty miserable rain-soaked miles back to the sawmill.

Three days later the storm had subsided enough for Capt. Sutter to make the journey. As he approached the sawmill a muddy, rain-soaked figure appeared from the nearby underbrush, angrily demanding why Sutter was three days late in arriving.

The stoutly built Captain was at last able to pacify his partner and together the two made their muddy way to the tailrace. The storm had served to wash away much of the dirt and gravel lining the channel. As they moved nearer they could hardly believe their eyes. Lining the seams of the tailrace, covering the area all around, were countless tiny golden flakes!

And so gold was discovered in California. When the discovery leaked out most of Sutter's and Marshall's friends and acquaintances (and almost all of the newspapers) refused to believe they had truly struck a bonanza. Many chose to believe that the two had made false claims of a gold strike to increase the values of their properties and to stimulate trade at their various enterprises.

On March 15, 1848, The San Francisco *Californian* ran a small article on the story as follows:

GOLD MINE FOUND

In the newly made raceway of the Sawmill recently erected by Captain Sutter, on the American Fork, gold has been found in considerable quantities. One person brought thirty dollars worth to New Helvetia, gathered there in a short time. California, no doubt, is rich in mineral wealth, great chances here for scientific capitalists. Gold has been found in almost every part of the country.

It was only natural that San Francisco's newspapers (and others) were slow to realize the importance of James Marshall's strike. They had received such news stories many times before. Previously such reports had proven false. But when at last Marshall's goldstrike was confirmed it was too late for the newspapers to set the record straight. For they were no longer able to publish! Gone were their reporters, their typesetters, their press operators; gone like most of the other males of the community to seek their fortunes with a shovel!

"Gold fever" spread like wildfire across the young nation and around the world. Grocery clerks laid aside their aprons and lawyers their Gladstones, while doctors, dentists, and men from *all* walks of life gave up their professions (often severing all ties) to head for California by the quickest means possible. The arrival of the multitudes changed San Francisco from a small, peaceful seaport into a roiling beehive of miners, merchants, gamblers, thieves and whores, each vying in his or her fashion for a share of the golddust wrested from the bowels of the motherlode country.

Waiting in the wings some three thousand miles to the east were two shrewd Yankee businessmen who watched with great interest as the drama of the gold country unfolded.

The elder of the two, Henry Wells, was born in Thetford, Vermont in the year 1805. As a boy he suffered from a speech impediment. This obstacle, which would have deterred many, served to give him even more drive and ambition. In 1836 he became the employee of a freight company serving the Erie Canal. His first job in the business was as freight and passenger forwarder. Then in 1841 Wells went to work for William F. Harndon, regarded by many as the "Father" of the express business. The ambitious young man soon approached Harndon with the idea of setting up a route to handle express between Albany and Buffalo. But the veteran turned down the proposition several times and finally advised Wells that if he wanted to see such a line established he "should do it himself." Shortly thereafter Wells resigned from Harndon's firm to carry out his plan. With Crawford Livingston and George E. Pomeroy he established Livingston, Wells and Pomeroy Company. They had not been operating for very long before learning how wise Harndon's refusal to service the area had been.

There can be no doubt that the many hardships Henry Wells faced during this period served to sharpen his business acumen to the highest degree and helped prepare him for the great business ventures lying ahead. Ironically, from this time on Wells' star began to soar ever higher and higher in the business world while that of Harndon's gradually dimmed and faded into oblivion.

William G. Fargo, born in 1818, was a native of Onandaga County, New York. He was one of seven brothers who entered the express business. Like Wells, he was extremely enterprising and energetic. For a while he served as first agent for the newly formed Auburn and Syracuse Railroad, leaving that position in 1842 to join Livingston, Wells, and Pomeroy Company where he first met Henry Wells. It was soon evident to his superiors that Fargo was an asset to their company. In a short time he and Wells became great friends and eventually (in 1845) formed a company known as Wells & Co. Western Express. Although Wells soon sold out his interest in that company to form Livingston, Wells, and Company, he left the partnership regretfully, such was his regard for young Fargo.

After the death of Crawford Livingston in 1847, Wells continued the business as Wells & Company. For two years he continued his operations and then reappraised the express business as clouds began to appear upon the horizon. It became increasingly clear to him that the express business was one which best lent itself to regional operation, rather than to fragmentation with small companies connecting with each other's lines in varying degrees of efficiency and responsibility or, in effect, needlessly duplicating facilities. This was brought home to him when the firm of Butterfield and Wasson entered into direct competition with Wells for the business between New York and Buffalo. The latter city was the connecting point with Livingston and Fargo's Western Express which at first ran to Detroit and then was extended to Chicago and other midwestern cities. Taking note of the advantages that could result from a combination of forces, and having the greatest of respect for the men in the other firms, he met with them to discuss their mutual problem. As a result the three firms merged into a powerful combine in the year 1850. Capitalized for $150,000, the new firm bore the name American Express Co. and had as its officers Henry Wells, president, William G. Fargo, secretary, and John Butterfield, line superintendent. Once again Henry Wells and William Fargo were reunited in the business that each of them knew and loved so well. Associated with them in the new company were some of the most reputable men in the express business, men, incidentally, with great financial backing.

While these events were transpiring along the Atlantic seaboard, the western goldslopes were being inundated with goldseekers. By the year 1850 over a hundred thousand men had reached the motherlode country. One year later their number had swollen to over three hundred thousand! It was only natural that their arrival created many problems overnight. Food supplies grew short; hardware, mining gear, and all other supplies were soon almost impossible to find. It was definitely a seller's market and prices (at first merely doubled or tripled) went sky high.

In such an atmosphere it became evident to several enterprising souls that a far greater fortune could be gleaned by supplying the needs and demands of the miners than by wielding a shovel on some barren claim.

Foremost among such thinkers was Alvin Adams, "north of Boston" Yankee. In 1840 Adams had been in the express business, "carrying commissions parcels in his hat." Within eight years he had become very successful and his companies, Adams' Eastern Express, Adams' Southern Express and Adams' Western Express were housed at No. 18, Wall Street. Now Adams beat all of his competition to the punch; on November 1, 1849, the steamship *Panama* rounded Clark's Point under Telegraph Hill. It had left the East Coast in September bearing 45,000 letters, several bales of newspapers and 320 passengers. Among them was Daniel Hale Haskell, one of Adam's employees entrusted to put Adams & Co. in business in California. Haskell moved quickly. Within nine days he had rented a small wooden building and set up his organization. The *Alta California* of November 8, 1849, stated the following bit of information;

> Gold dust bought, also forwarded to any of the above places, and bills of exchange given in any amounts. Letter-bags made up and forwarded by a special messenger in each of the steamers.

Overnight Adams & Co. had expanded its operation and was no longer just an express company. Now, by a new policy of buying gold it took the first of a succession of steps which brought it fully into the banking business in California. At the same time it added another dimension by engaging in the carrying of mail.

One of the early companies was set up by Alexander Todd in 1849. Originally Todd had reached San Francisco intending to work the mines. But soon he realized his health was not up to the strenuous work required, so he cast about for an alternate means of making a living. Overnight he had his answer. Noting the problems of mail delivery to the men who were far from home and eager for any and all news from their loved ones, Todd rode horseback throughout the southern motherlode country recording the names of every miner who wanted his mail delivered. Each miner paid Todd one dollar as a recording fee and gave him an ounce of gold dust for each letter delivered. Overnight Todd's new business was booming and he had over 2,000 miners signed for the mail delivery. Soon he was carrying gold dust, passengers and freight. He operated until September of 1853 when he sold out to Wells, Fargo & Co.

Contrary to what would be expected, the pioneer expressman-mail carrier bore a charmed life. Due to the great concern of all the miners about getting their mail and packages "from back East," highwaymen and bandits didn't dare touch the messengers. They were wise. Had there been any serious holdups of the carriers it was generally believed that miners everywhere would have dropped their shovels, hunted down the bandits and hung them from the nearest tree.

As time went by the mining industry was changing. At first the operation had been simple. The discovery and "diggin'" of the precious yellow metal had depended upon lonely miners who stalked the mountains and countryside with pick, shovel, cradle and pan. Now that was being changed with the use of the "long tom," an extended cradle which replaced the simple type rocker. In 1851 the dredger made its appearance and hydraulic gold mining began. Later improvements were the shaft drill, the stamp mill and other revolutionary measures which led to placer mining and deep mines.

As a result of the growth and development of the mining industry the express companies were forced to expand to keep pace. Those that were able to do so prospered greatly, among them Adams & Co. which was now the largest express company on the Pacific Coast. Not only did the company ship messages by land and sea, it also provided a "special messenger" whose job was to guard and protect his messages against flood, fire, sinking of a ship and outlaws.

In the year 1851 some $60,000,000 in gold reached the East from the Pacific Coast! *And Adams and Co. had carried most of it!* It is said that when this news reached the ears of Henry Wells and William Fargo they called a meeting of the officers of the American Express Company to establish a branch of the company in California and get their share of the lucrative business. But reportedly John Butterfield and two others on the board vetoed such an expansion, based on the theory that "the gold rush could hardly last!"

Wells and Fargo mulled the situation over, carefully considering all possibilities. It is indicative of their shrewd business sense that they decided to risk such an adventure outside the corporate framework of American Express. Plans were made, meetings with key financial people were held and on March 18, 1852, a joint stock company was organized under the general incorporation laws of New York. Capitalized at $300,000, its principal backers were Henry Wells, William Fargo, Johnston Livingston, and E.B. Morgan.

Following the founding of the new corporation Samuel P. Carter was named to set up the forwarding part of the business in California, while R.W. Washburn, a banker, was appointed to establish the banking department of Wells, Fargo and Company in San Francisco.

The stage was set. On May 20, 1852, the first public announcement regarding the newly founded corporation was announced in the *New York Times:*

WELLS, FARGO & CO. CALIFORNIA EXPRESS

CAPITAL $300,000

A joint stock company   Office 16 Wall Street

Directors

Henry Wells, Johnston Livingston, Elijah P. Williams,
Edwin B. Morgan, Wm. G. Fargo, Jas. McKay,
Alpheus Reynolds, Alex M.C. Smith, Henry D. Rice.

Edwin B. Morgan, President

James McKay, Secretary

This company having completed its organization
as above is now ready to undertake the general forwarding agency and commission business; the purch-
ase and sale of gold dust, bullion and specie, also
packages, parcels and freight of all description in and
between the City of New York and the City of San
Francisco, and the principal cities and towns in
California, connecting at New York with the lines of
the American Express Company, the Harnden Express, Pullen, Virgil and Co. European Express.

They have established offices and faithful agents
in all the principal cities and towns throughout the
eastern, middle and western states, energetic and
faithful messengers furnished with iron chests for the
security of treasure and other valuable packages ac-
company each express upon all their lines as well as in
California and in the Atlantic States.

Samuel P. Carter, for many years connected with
the American Express, and R. W. Washburn, late of
the Bank of Syracuse, have been appointed principal
agents in California.

Samuel Carter arrived at San Francisco June 27, 1852.
On July 2, the *Herald* carried a public announcement
concerning the new company and added a footnote of
their own further endorsing the list of directors:

A glance at the list of directors will satisfy anyone of
the unlimited confidence which may be reposed in
the establishment.

Reuben W. Washburn arrived in San Francisco two weeks after Carter by means of the steamer *Tennessee,* carrying sixty-five packages which are said to have been the first shipment by Wells Fargo between the Atlantic and Pacific states. Starting July 11th the San Francisco office received regular semi-monthly shipments from the east and, from July 30th on, it obliged by sending shipments out of San Francisco regularly.

Endowed with canny leadership, the new company looked about, evaluating its competitors. In November of 1852 it announced the acquisition of Gregory and Company's Express, the first of many such moves. Such a move not only eliminated a competitor in that particular area but also put Wells Fargo in control of a route doing good business between Stockton, Sacramento and San Francisco. Soon afterward, in September 1853, Wells Fargo bought out Todd and Company Express; then, July 24, 1854, acquired Hunter and Company Express. Indicative of their great business acumen is the fact that the acquisition of these three companies enabled Wells Fargo to blanket all parts of the Mother Lode and, that taken care of, the company could concentrate on the establishment of new offices in southern California and other parts of the state.

Soon Wells Fargo had offices throughout the mining areas and in all the larger trading centers. Certain of the larger offices were designated both express and banking agencies, as, for instance, in 1856 the offices at Sacramento, Stockton, Marysville, and Portland, Oregon, as well as both the New York and San Francisco headquarters. The remaining offices, some sixty of them, including offices in Panama and Honolulu, in 1856 were designated as express agencies, only. In all the offices however, the operation was the same; the miner could bring his gold dust, have it weighed on very delicate scales, and obtain the company's signed receipt for it. The entire operation was straightforward and simple, and the miners liked the way that Wells Fargo stood behind their word.

As time went by Wells Fargo bought up the various stagecoach lines carrying its freight, and by 1866 owned the largest stagecoach system in the entire world. As various goldfields were discovered the company continued to expand, eventually having more offices and facilities in Arizona, Nevada, Idaho, Montana and Oregon.

The San Francisco headquarters was established in the year 1852. Built by Sam Brannan, a Mormon, it was located just across from the Parrot Building which housed their rival, Adams & Co. at the northwest corner of Montgomery and California Streets.

The basic structure of Wells Fargo underwent some changes as time went by. Originally the express and banking departments were housed in the same building and usually did their advertising together. The two departments and their bookkeeping had been kept separate, however, from the very first. In the hey-day of the company's stagecoaching a separate stage department was organized to manage that activity. In California's disastrous financial crisis of 1855, some of Wells Fargo's banking offices were closed for from one to several days, while the company took stock of its position, but it was fully sound, quickly resumed its banking, while express operation had not been interrupted.

In the early days of the gold rush the shipping companies had handled most of the West Coast's imports and exports. But California's remoteness from the manufacturing centers created great problems for the delivery of goods. Normally, from three to six months were required for a ship to travel from New York to San Francisco by way of Cape Horn and deliver its eagerly awaited cargo. But the increasing competition among the express companies resulted in great changes. Soon freight was being transported from New York to San Francisco across the Isthmus of Panama—*in less than 34 days!* True, the cost was higher, but the extra costs were offset by the great savings in interest on the money invested in the merchandise. Another plus was the rapid turnover of the goods. Soon all kinds of goods such as "perishables" were reaching the West Coast by the new route. Needless to say the miners were happy to pay more in order to have some of the luxuries that they had done without for so long. It was a seller's market and the seller usually took advantage of that fact, except for the rare occasion when over-ordering brought market gluts and temporary low prices.

Naturally freight costs were very high during those years. According to records, Adams & Co. charged as much as 75¢ per pound for freight shipped between New York and San Francisco. But with the entry of Wells Fargo in the western arena Adams dropped their prices to 60¢ and later to 40¢ per pound.

The concern with which Wells Fargo regarded its public trust is revealed in the following instructions issued by the company to one of its special messengers:

> You are furnished by us, on leaving here, with a list of all our Express goods going with you and also of all the Trunks and Bags in your immediate charge—of which Trunks and Bags you will take especial care until you arrive at San Francisco and deliver the same only to persons connected with our office there.
>
> Take no packages from others either here or on the route unless for Consuls or officers of the Steamship Company.
>
> In no case nor under any consideration whatever, let any package, or letter or letters which we have put under your immediate charge go out of your care until you deliver the same to persons connected with our San Francisco office as after herein directed.
>
> While on way up on Pacific side, prepare a careful Alphabetical list of all San Francisco (City) Letters in your Bag, make it on the headed sheets we give you (dating each sheet). Get the Purser's Report and put it and your letter list in Letter Bag, and when nearing San Francisco our News Boat (with Flat and Capt. Martin on board) will come off-then throw Bag Let-

ters and Bag Newspapers to him: be ready for him so as not to miss fire.

Report yourself with Trunks as soon as possible to our folks in San Francisco Look for our wagon on the dock and go up in it, losing no time.

Directly related to the delivery of parcels by the express companies was the delivery of letters. The services originally initiated by such pioneers as Alexander Todd were continued by the larger firms that followed. In the gold country the populace preferred their mail to be delivered by the express companies; experience had proven that the express firms had a far better record of deliveries and service. But government opposition soon arose. The *Alta California* ran the following notice in its January 13, 1854 edition:

> J.D. FRY, Esq. Special Agent of the Post Office Dept., has given us official notice that all letters sent by our expresses hereafter, must bear the Post Office Stamp or Envelope.
>
> Wells, Fargo & Co.
> Adams & Co.

Public resentment was immediately forthcoming as a result of the above notice. The *California Chronicle* ran a disapproving article containing the following statement:

> . . . it would be next to impossible to carry on business without expresses, this command is not only burdensome, but tyrannical.

Despite the government restrictions the letter-carrying operation continued to be very lucrative for Wells Fargo and for Adams & Co.

Generally speaking, in the early 1850s the traffic in gold dust was the greatest source of profit for the western express companies, but the margin between their buying price and the price they obtained at the mint progressively narrowed as time went on.

In the fall of 1852 Henry Wells decided to make a trip "out west" and see for himself what was happening. He journeyed by way of the Isthmus of Panama and when he finally arrived in San Francisco he was elated to see his company's progress.

Proudly Henry Wells made the tour of various Wells Fargo offices, watching the company's tellers as they waited on their customers, weighing dust at the shiny brass scales and performing other services. He nodded with approval as his canny eyes observed the rapidly rising share of business Wells Fargo was winning away from its competitors.

When at last Henry Wells returned East, it was with a great feeling of achievement and satisfaction in the company's western adventure. It was a trip that he would never forget and his glowing reports strongly influenced Wells Fargo's directors to authorize "full steam ahead" for the firm's expansion on the Pacific Coast. One does not know what his report might have been had he made his trip two years later when the West Coast was engulfed in the great financial panic of '55. Perhaps he still would have recognized Wells Fargo's strong points and the future that lay ahead, but it would have taken courage and foresight aplenty to be optimistic about California in 1855.

CHAPTER
II

LOUIS REMME'S
RIDE

Louis Remme felt just great! Things had worked out mighty well, after all. The cattle had sold good; all told, he had deposited $12,500 with Adams and Company. He patted the pocket of his coat where the receipt was riding, reassured by the slight bulkiness that it made. Its touch gave him a feeling of security, knowing that his future was now secure. A man could do a lot with that kind of money!

Louis Remme felt inside his coat pocket and pulled out a long-nine. Carefully he nibbled at the end of the cigar, then dragged a match across the sole of his boot and applied the flame to the tobacco. He drew deep, enjoying the bite of the weed. Yeah, after all the work and worry of the past several years, things were looking up. Life could be good, after all!

His thoughts were broken as he looked up through the drifting gray haze to see his host bearing down upon him, a fresh copy of the *Sacramento Union* in his hand.

The cattleman settled deep in the cushions of the heavy leather chair and started reading the news, scanning past the numerous advertisements lauding the merits of patent medicines, tobaccos, and men's celluloid collars. He was half finished with his cigar when he saw the item. Suddenly whole lines of black type seemed to leap out of the pages at him. "ADAMS AND COMPANY CLOSE DOORS!" . . . "MANAGING DIRECTOR WOODS HAS FLOWN!" . . . "PAGE AND BACON HAVE FAILED!"

Suddenly Louis Remme was on his feet, hurrying out the ornate doors and heading down the street to Adams and Company. He felt a sinking sensation in his stomach as he turned a corner and saw the mob clamoring in front of the express and banking office. Not a tall man, he stretched to his full height of five-foot-nine and plunged into the mass of humanity, ignoring the angry protests as he pushed forward.

Loudly Remme shouted, trying to make himself heard over the noise of the mob, "Here! Here! This is my certificate for twelve-thousand, five-hundred dollars. I'll take my money now!"

Wearily the clerk stared down at the cattleman. Shaking his head, he leaned down, shouting in Remme's ear. "Sorry, sir. Wish I could help you. But see that line?" He pointed to the angry men. "They all want their money. My advice to you is to stay right here until the receiver comes. Maybe he — "

The man's words faded as Louis Remme plunged away, his mind working as he sought an answer to his plight. Could he get his money at San Francisco? No, the *Sacramento Union* had got its information from a San Francisco paper. No, there'd been such a run there that no money was left. He had to get to one of the outlying Adams and Company offices, one that had not yet got the news of the company's disaster.

Suddenly he stopped in his tracks. Portland! That was it! It was so far away from San Francisco that they would not have gotten the bad news yet. And there was no telegraph serving the town, either. Yes, if he could beat the news there he stood a good chance of saving his hard-earned stake. But how? If he went to San Francisco and rode the next day's steamer he would arrive at the same time as the bad news.

He was standing there mulling his problem when he

22

saw the way out. Quickly he turned and ran for the river. Huffing and puffing from his effort, he jumped aboard the stern-wheeled river paddler just as it pulled up its gangplank and prepared to make way for Knight's Landing, forty-two miles upriver.

At Knight's Landing, Knight himself loaned him the horse that he rode to the head of Grand Island. There Judge Diefendorf, one of his oldest friends, fixed him up with a fresh mount and Louis Remme was starting one of the most spectacular endurance rides of all time!

It was almost sundown when he neared Marysville. Remme changed horses whenever it was possible. Luckily he was in country where he had a lot of friends; that made it easier to find good horseflesh. He continued in the saddle, pausing only to get a new mount and a hasty word of direction where he was not sure of the trail.

He was seventy hours from Knight's Landing when he reached Yreka. Then, dig the spurs and make Hungry Creek, Bear Creek, and finally Jacksonville. He entered the small village of Eugene on the fifth day and at the following sunrise galloped into French Prairie. By now he was so tired that he couldn't stay awake. Luckily he had been given a horse that knew its way. From time to time he dozed as it ran down the section line, lather flecking its neck and belly.

The sun was high above when he loped into Portland. Immediately the weary stockman spurred his mount to the building housing Adams and Company. Brushing himself off, he forced a look of casualness as he strolled through the door and eased up to the teller's window. He handed the man his certificate. Carefully the clerk studied the signature on the receipt, nodded his head and began to heap up gold coins. Presently he had put forty pounds of pure gold into a gunny sack, which he pushed to Remme. Remme smiled at the man, gave him one of his long-nines and left the office.

Shortly after Remme had cashed his certificate, he heard a cannon boom. The *Columbia* was just arriving from

San Francisco. An hour later she would be docking and men scrambling over the sides to run for the offices of Adams and Company, hoping to redeem the money they had with the bankrupt firm. Louis Remme headed for a hotel, his head, shoulders and entire body sagging with fatigue. Damn, he was tired! But he slept well, knowing his money was safe!

He had ridden 665 miles in 143 hours, total time. Ten of those hours he had spent in sleeping. Over all he had averaged a speed of about five miles per hour through rains, storms, mudslides and Indians. The gutsy cattleman would long be remembered for his dramatic ride!

As Wells Fargo prospered and grew, its quarters in San Francisco became too crowded. The executives looked around, then considered renting vacant offices in Sam Brannan's Express Building. The Express Building was across the street from the Parrott Building where Adams and Company had their offices.

The Parrott Building was the first in San Francisco to be built of stone. Erected by John Parrott, a wealthy banker who'd made his fortune in Mazatlan, it had a unique history. All of the stone used in the edifice had been bought and cut in far-off China, then shipped to San Francisco. Despite the shipping costs, Parrott had saved money by buying the stone in China rather than in the United States.

In due time the stone arrived in San Francisco and was delivered to the site, located at the northwest corner of Montgomery and California Streets. All went well until the contractor started the building. Then he learned that every stone was "keyed" by Chinese symbols.

Exasperated, Parrott sent to China for the Chinese foreman who had been the overseer during the cutting of the stone. But when the man arrived, he looked at the site and the stone and shook his head. He told Parrott he was putting the building on the wrong corner. There, he explained, the building would be subjected to evil spirits, and the gods would not let the building or its tenants prosper! He pointed to the northeast corner and said it had been cut for *that* corner!

But Parrott had already bought the lot on the northwest corner and was not about to change locations. Eventually he got the building finished. His tenants moved in and opened for business. But not one Chinese would enter the building!

In January of 1854 Wells Fargo moved into the Express Building. It had been raised on the spot where the Chinese foreman had suggested John Parrott build his building in 1852. It was soon apparent that the Chinese were aware of what was happening in the business world. Each day, for a long time, long lines of Chinese gathered and passed slowly and ceremoniously through the bank, paying their respects to Taoi Pah Shing Kwun, their god of wealth. And each day, there were numerous new Chinese depositors. . . The Chinese had the utmost confidence in Wells Fargo's integrity.

There was a financial downswing through the United States in the latter part of 1854. For some time the financial clouds had been darkening, due to rash spending, misuse of credit, overspeculation in stocks and bonds, and other ill-advised ventures.

One such venture that would soon take its toll was the Ohio and Mississippi Railroad project. For some time there had been a tendency of big money to invest in railroads feeling that they were a "sure thing." That had been the feeling of Page and Bacon Co. of St. Louis when they started pouring money into the Ohio and Mississippi. But the railroad had many problems. Now Page and Bacon were in so deep that they couldn't stop. They were depleting their cash reserves and were beginning to feel the pinch.

Wells Fargo, ever with an ear to the ground, became aware of Page, Bacon & Co's troubles. Anticipating what would eventually happen, the heads of Wells Fargo began a policy of keeping an extremely large cash reserve available. How shrewd that decision was would shortly be seen! In California things generally were on the down side. Commenting on the problems of the day, the *Daily Placer Times and Transcript* said:

> In a commercial point of view, the news which goes forward by the steamer today is of the most discouraging character. Trade is utterly prostrate, and the pecuniary embarrassments of the mercantile classes have never been equalled since the settlement of the country by the Anglo-Americans. The principal cause producing this state of things has frequently before been alluded to by us the absence of sufficient rain to enable the miners to prosecute their labors.

Mining methods had changed greatly as gold became harder to find. The placer miner depended on running water to wash and work the gravel; the drought and lack of rain was disastrous!

When Christmas arrived in '54 shopping was way down, unemployment up, and several mercantile firms across the country went broke.

But despite the general trend, Wells Fargo was still prospering. John Q. Jackson, Wells Fargo agent of Auburn, released figures revealing that his company was shipping about $2,000,000 annually from the five offices located in Auburn, Yankee Jim's, Iowa Hill, Michigan Bluff, and Rattlesnake Bar. The company was growing. By 1854 it had twenty-four offices, scattered across (and serving) the most profitable area of the gold country. And, in September, it paid an extra 5% dividend, making a total of 15% in declared dividends for the year.

The blow that triggered the panic of '55 came in February of that year. Page and Bacon Co. of St. Louis had hopelessly overextended themselves, trying to keep the Ohio and Mississippi Railroad project alive. Suddenly the railroad went "belly up." Overnight its failure brought down not only the firm's St. Louis house but also its associated banking firm in San Francisco. From that day forth, it was simply a case of the "domino theory" all over again!

When the steamship *Oregon* arrived at San Francisco, February 18, 1855, it brought news of the St. Louis banking firm's failure. Immediately investors swarmed upon Page, Bacon of California, demanding their money from its coffers. Unfortunately for them (and the bank too) the firm had sent $1,000,000 to the parent bank in St. Louis just a few days before. There was very little cash on hand and it was quickly wiped out. On February 22, the bank closed its doors.

The next day, known ever since as "Black Friday," brought about the closing of most of the city's banking institutions. Adams and Company, A.S. Wright Company (a private banker), Robinson and Company, Wells Fargo, all closed their doors. The "run" had depleted their cash on hand.

When the news hit the gold fields similar conditions existed. . . .

At Auburn, Adams and Company closed early Friday morning, but armed citizens forced their cashier to reopen and pay off depositors until their vault was empty.

At Nevada City, Adams and Company paid off some favored investors, then closed their doors.

In Stockton, sheriffs waited with attachment papers as the stages came back from the mines. All gold found in the stagecoaches was seized for distribution by the courts later.

At Jamestown a mob broke into Adams and Company's offices, opened the vault and found it empty.

And at Sonora, a mob stormed Adams and Company and took $49,000. It was claimed later that most of the mob were not depositors, but had joined in the break-in for the thrill of it. While a small portion of the money was being distributed to legitimate depositors, some lawyers collected a percentage of that money as their fees for dropping attachment proceedings they had initiated.

I.C. Woods, Adams' partner, fled from the state in the middle of the night. It was learned that he had "feathered his nest" by using company money to build the port town of Ravenwood and a nearby farm (located in present day Menlo Park) called Woodside Dairy. In addition, Woods had hidden gold in the walls of a frame and mud house that he owned.

San Francisco was staggered! Drastic fires had caused the financial community severe losses in 1850 and '51. Now, one hundred and ninety-seven businesses were forced to close their doors, with liabilities of approximately $8,000,000.

The effect upon the morale of the people was devastating; their confidence in banks and financial institutions was shattered. . .

On Sunday morning, February 25, an article in the *Alta* announced:

> Wells, Fargo & Co. have completed a balance of their accounts this day, and find to the credit of their house above every liability, $389,105.23; and only ask of their friends a few days to convert some of their assets, to resume payment.

The effect upon the people was electrifying! Wells Fargo had come through with flying colors! From that day on the company was hailed by depositors, newspapers and countless thousands as the epitome of financial institutions. And, its depositors grew daily.

Such was the company's rapid expansion that they were soon overcrowded in the Express Building. The Parrott Building, formerly occupied by the bankrupts, Adams and Company, and Page, Bacon & Co., was now empty. In the summer of 1856 Wells Fargo moved into John Parrott's supposedly jinxed building, arranged for a delegation of Chinese to perform rites exorcising the evil spirits, and renamed it the Wells Fargo Building. (It is interesting that throughout the panic of '55 the Chinese had such faith in Taoi Pah Shing Kwun, their god of wealth, and Wells Fargo, that they left their money in the bank.)

During the panic the express houses of Wells Fargo had carried on "business as usual." Some of the former Adams employees started a new company to compete with Wells Fargo, but they couldn't make a go of it and before long fell by the wayside. The financial debacle of 1855 brought Wells Fargo into a dominant position in both banking and express on the Pacific Coast.

Typical of the company's image following the dark days of the panic, are the following two articles. The first, from the *Shasta Courier,* concerned the opening of a new office in the northern counties:

> Messrs. Wells Fargo & Co., our readers will be informed by reference to our advertising columns, are about establishing a branch of their very popular house in this place. During the financial explosion a few months back, Wells Fargo & Co. stood the shock without exhibiting the least quivering. They have, in consequence, the confidence of the entire commercial portion of the state. They have also, by their promptness and FIDELITY in attending all business entrusted to them, won for themselves a name as expressmen that is of itself the highest encomium that

can be paid to their deserts. S. Knight is to be the resident in this place. Judging from a very short acquaintance with the gentleman, we are inclined to the opinion that he is possessed of one of the requisites of a good expressman, at least; that of being a good, clever gentleman.

A fire in Grass Valley resulted in the following article:

A fire broke out in the United States Hotel and rapidly spread to the adjoining buildings. The vault of Wells Fargo & Company withstood the hottest of the fire and preserved its valuable contents. The loss was especially great because the merchants had just laid in large stocks of goods for the fall trade . . . the most notable example of energy of action was that of A. Delano, agent for Wells, Fargo & Company. About an hour after the astonished sun had gazed upon the scene of desolation, a frame shanty was seen moving down the hill from the west end of the town. Slowly but surely it advanced and was backed up against Wells, Fargo & Company's brick vault, which was still standing among the ruins. In a few moments "Old Block" appeared with a sign on which was painted, "Wells, Fargo & Co.'s Express Office." In less than eight hours after the cry of fire had alarmed the midnight air, "Old Block" stood smiling behind his counter, amid the smouldering ruins and with the ground still warm beneath his feet, ready, as he said, "to attend to business."

In 1855 Wells Fargo paid dividends of 5% on two different occasions and the company's capital was increased to $600,000. And, only seven months after "Black Friday," the company had 40 express offices on the Pacific Coast from San Diego to Portland, Oregon, plus its offices in New York, Panama, and Honolulu. In October, Louis McLane was appointed the head of Wells Fargo's California operation. An enterprising man, he would one day be the company's president.

It has been estimated that by 1852 the gold country stretched 180 miles from north to south, and covered about 20,000 square miles. It included all, or parts of, Amador, Calaveras, El Dorado, Mariposa, Merced, Placer, Tuolumne, and Yuba Counties. The rich lodes were found along the foothills of the Sierras, and in the valleys of the American, Feather, Sacramento and the Yuba Rivers; other important amounts of gold were found along parts of the Cosumnes, Mokelumne, Calaveras, Stanislaus, Tuolumne, and Merced Rivers.

One of the biggest problems of the miner was keeping this gold after he had grubbed the earth for it. He could pile up his gold dust and amass a fortune, but how was he to get the benefits of it? The mint was far away, transportation across the rough mountains was risky, and always compounded by the possibility of outlaws and road agents.

That's where Wells Fargo entered the picture. Its operation was to deliver the miner's packages, letters and newspapers, as well as weigh, assay and protect his gold. And finally, they shipped it anywhere in the world that he desired or, in exchange for it, would issue him a draft, that is, a check upon the company, which could conveniently be enclosed in an envelope and sent to its destination by U.S. mail or by Wells Fargo's private mail service, which for many years was faster and safer and extremely popular with the public.

On the average the miner did not make much money. He had to work hard or be lucky to make a living. With prices as high as they were he had a tough row to hoe. Flour was $100 a barrel, bread $1 per loaf (when it was to be had), whiskey $16 per bottle, molasses $6 a gallon, and nails $5 a pound. For $1 a miner could get a shirt laundered; sometimes shirts actually were sent to China for this service due to a shortage of laundry facilities in the gold camps.

The miner never needed a clock. His working hours were from daylight to dark, and his time was spent in backbreaking labor, digging, carrying water, and building sluiceways and dams. He earned whatever rewards he could coax from the earth!

There was little diversion in his life. Work had first priority. But when he did manage to get a few dollars ahead, or make a strike, most miners headed for the saloon. It was the gathering place where men from the diggin's got together to reminisce about other places, other times and their loved ones back home. And if he drank a little too much and talked a little too loud, that was his business. Unless he went too far—that was something else!

Law, generally speaking, was something a man wore on his hip. But there were times when the men of the camp banded together to dispense justice to some thief who had stolen a fellow miner's dust, horse, or life. Typical of the gold camp newspapers is the following item:

> A miner's jury was formed last evening to render a decision in the trial of Pete Jones who was accused of shooting Tom Winters in the back. The jury found against Jones. Following the hanging the jury retired to the Goldstrike saloon for refreshments. Jones died well.

1856 was another year marked by progress and growth for Wells Fargo. Twenty-three new offices were opened including some with such strange sounding names as Chinese Camp, Drytown, Indian Diggin's, Martinez, and Ophir. The company was spreading out, opening new offices at the rate of one every three weeks.

The following year was fraught with many problems for the United States. There was a lack of rainfall, crops were very poor, and an epidemic of grasshoppers plagued the Midwest. In the West, gold production dropped far below the usual standards.

Another factor causing a great part of the nation's financial trouble was the overcapitalization and overbuilding of railroads. It seems that they had not learned the lessons of the panic of '55.

The panic of 1857 started on October 23rd. . . A large

commercial firm in New York closed on that date and immediately others in nearby Boston, Toronto, Cincinnati, and St. Louis toppled and fell. The news traveled through the country, undermining the economic structure, and banks, financial instiutions, and businesses of all kinds threw in the towel. By November 3rd, the country was at a standstill.

Perhaps the one bright spot was in San Francisco and the Gold Country. There they had put in practice the things garnered from the rough days of 1855.

Wells Fargo rolled along pretty much as usual and early in 1857 judged that the California economy had improved to a degree justifying again a stepping up of its lending activities.

The Gods of Fortune had smiled down upon the Gold Country . . . within the first dozen years following James Marshal's fateful discovery, the fruitful earth had "birthed" $585,000,000 worth of the precious yellow gold. Wells Fargo alone had hauled approximately $59,000,000 in from the mines in the years from 1852 through 1858.

As the forty-niners hurried westward over the rough topography then known as "western Utah," little did they suspect the vast wealth that lay beneath them, wealth that would one day cause many of them to retrace their footsteps to one of the richest bonanzas of all—the fabulous Comstock Lode!

Gold had first been discovered in Gold Hill and Six-Mile Canyon (north and west of Carson City) in 1850, but the strike had not been a rich one. Only a handful of "ragpickin'" miners had stayed on to work the area.

Two brothers, Hosea and Ethan Allen Grosch, from Pennsylvania, were the first to have any inkling of the bonanza waiting beneath the rough, boulder-strewn crust of their claim. As they worked their "diggin'" their tempers were always riled by the thick, gray, sticky "goo" that clung to their picks and shovels, making digging almost impossible. In a letter to their father, Parson Grosch, they described the matter as looking somewhat like "thin-sheet lead," or maybe "carbonate of silver."

One day in 1853 the brothers crossed the mountains to Downieville and had a sample of the worrisome "goo" assayed. Supposedly they were quite stunned when they got the assayer's report. They returned home, built a small smelting furnace, and starting charting the entire area. During this time they were quite secretive, and made notes continuously in their notebooks; notebooks that were never shown to anyone.

But the brothers were not destined to reap the fruits of their discovery. Tragedy befell them. Soon Hosea was dead from blood-poisoning, caused by a wound from a miner's pick. Ethan Allen made a great mistake in judgement, gambling that he could cross the Sierras in winter; he was wrong, and he died in a blizzard. Behind them the brothers left their claim, furnace, charts, and notebooks; they also left a caretaker. He was Henry P.T. (Old Pancake) Comstock. And one day his name would be identified with one of the richest bonanzas of all.

June 11th, 1859, started out to be another weary, back breaking day as Pat McLaughlin and Pete O'Riley worked their claim near the little mining camp. As usual, they griped as they had to pause every few minutes to dig the thick gray "goo" from their shovels. Suddenly they stopped, eyes wide-open and staring . . . They had hit a solid ledge of quartz! Excitedly they were down on their knees, checking their find. It was true! They had really hit a strike! Excitedly they spread the news.

Little did they know then what they had discovered. Their claim, later to be known as the Ophir Mine, would eventually yield $145,000,000 of the precious metals. And the ore at the surface of their claim would prove to be worth $1,595 per ton in gold, and $4,791 per ton in silver! The news of the sensational strike rang through Sun Peak's saloons and echoed throughout the Sierras. Not only did Sun Peak have gold, it had silver, too!

From the date of James Marshal's discovery, it had taken a year for the California goldfields to gain momen-

tum. Not so with Nevada. The men, tools, machinery and supplies needed to reap its bountiful harvest were ready and waiting just over the Sierras in California, waiting for just such a strike as Sun Peak, Gold Hill and Six-Mile Canyon proved to be. With the news of the discovery, every miner who hadn't yet made his stake, every road agent who'd worn out his welcome along the stagecoach trails of the Motherlode country, and every money-seeking businessman, harlot, and tinhorn gambler grabbed the first transportation possible and headed for the new fields!

They came by way of horseback, teams and wagons, stagecoach, and even by carts and wagons pulled by plodding teams of oxen, Get there and dig, boy. It was just layin' there, waitin' fer you!

Someone said that California packed up and headed for Nevada . . .

Sun Peak underwent a name change. One night when the camp was roaring, one of its town characters, grizzled "Old Virginny" Finney (or Fenimore) stumbled and fell while deep in his cups and smashed the bottle he was carrying. Owlishly he stared at the bottle and the other drunks standing around, then hiccupped, "I christen this here town Virginia." And Virginia City it was from that time on.

It was said to be the rowdiest no-holds-barred camp of them all. Alvin Harlow gives a vivid description of Virginia City's greatest hour in his highly interesting book, *Old Waybills:*

> Virginia City in the first three years of the '60's was in a fever of development—houses being thrown up with frantic haste, stamp mills thundering and belching smoke, stores jammed with buyers and making a hundred per cent profit on every sale, auctioneers yelling, newspapers dashing off extras, fire companies clanging to and fro, saloons open day and night, hurdy gurdies, theaters and dancehalls all alight and humming with activity, stage-coaches with

cracking whips and "yip-yip-yipping" clattering through the crowded streets amid flying dust and gravel, pulling up with a flourish at the door of the Wells, Fargo or other office to discharge passengers, bags of mail and bags of gold.

Indeed, Virginia City was a heller! Seventy-two hundred feet above sea level, built on the side of a steep mountain, there would sometimes be as much as a fifty foot drop from one of its dog legged streets to another. With the advent of the new gold-seekers, the little mining town's population soared from practically nothing to over twenty thousand within the first twelve months!

A mint would be established soon in nearby Carson City to process the precious metal; in 1864 the rough, raw territory would be admitted to statehood; and the course of the Civil War would be greatly affected as Nevada's silver and gold flowed into the Union coffers, infusing them with new life!

And Wells Fargo was there . . . on the ground floor, as usual; there to provide the struggling miner with the services he needed so desperately; the delivery of his mail, freight, and newspapers; the shipping and often bloody safeguarding of his hard-gained yellow dust; services that time and the panics of '55 and '57 had proven were best rendered by Wells Fargo.

During the years ahead, the dynamic young company would continue shipping everything from mining tools and equipment, raw oysters, cut flowers for the dancehall girls, and other necessities (and luxuries) into the "diggin's." The Virginia City office, during the years of the Comstock Lode, would prove a tremendous source of business for Wells Fargo, and a few years later, would lead the company to buy and operate the Pioneer Stage Line over the Sierra, thereby adding a new, vital dimension to its vast empire!

CHAPTER
III

THE
CONCORD
COACH

With the Gold Rush of 1849 thousands of miners swarmed into the Motherlode country; the need for transportation and communication between the far-flung gold camps and the population centers of coastal and central California became greater and greater. Although the river network served the needs of a few of the newcomers, for most it was catch-as-catch-can; soon the demand for horses, mules, buggies and rigs sent prices sky high, forcing many of the late arrivals to travel by shank's mare.

The hue and cry for some means of transportation triggered the birth of California's stage lines in the year 1849. One of the earliest such ventures was that of John Whistman's Company whose battered old French coach initiated service between San Francisco and San Jose. Only nine hours was required for each run between the two settlements. Considering all the obstacles existing that was, indeed, very good time.

One of the early lines was Hall and Crandall's. Controlled by Berford's Express Company, the line operated from a San Francisco office and covered the area southward to San Jose. In later years the Hall and Crandall-Berford line bragged that their experienced drivers "make the quickest time and never meet with accidents, which are so likely with the old-fashioned stagecoaches." If such claims were true, the company's safety record was more likely due to the fact that they operated on the flatlands instead of in the mountain regions where snows, rainstorms, rockslides and treacherous narrow trails made stagecoaching a truly hazardous undertaking!

During August and September of 1850, advertisements in the Sacramento newspapers advised to the populace that James E. Birch's stages were carrying passengers and freight to Mormon Island, Georgetown, Coloma, Hangtown and Weaverville, and that letters and packages for those gold camps could be left for pickup at Henly, McKnight and Company's Express office. Birch, a Rhode Island stageman, arrived in '49 at the age of 21, and shortly afterwards was operating a stage line between the Coloma goldcamp and Sacramento. The cost of such a ride behind young Birch—in a rough wagon pulled by four wild Mexican mustangs with the aid of a bullwhip—was two ounces of gold dust or approximately $32. Birch's business grew and during the next few years he imported many stagecoaches into the mining country.

Another pioneer, Frank S. Stevens, founded the Pioneer Stage Line in 1851. It served the area from Sacramento to Placerville (Hangtown) and eventually linked the Overland Mail system from Sacramento as far east as Virginia City, Nevada.

In 1852 Johnson's Opposition Line advertised: "Through in 18 hours in new, first-class coaches—Leaving Colusa every day on arrival of steamers from San Francisco and Sacramento." On this same line Rhodes and Lusk's Express traveled, carrying "treasure, letters and packages weekly from San Francisco to Yreka, touching at intermediate points." Other companies entering the stage line business in the early days included Baxter and Company who ran north to the Oregon line, and Adams and Company who started operating from Sonora to Stockton in the middle of 1852.

Most of the early stage lines made their runs over rough trails that had never been graded or improved in any fashion. Wandering to and fro through the gold country, following the easiest, but seldom the shortest, path across creeks, rivers and perilous mountainsides, the majority of the routes left much to be desired. At times it was even necessary for passengers including women to get out and help push when their vehicle was bogged to the axles in mud or winter snow.

On some runs there were no stage stations between the gold camps. At such times passengers either "packed a lunch" or went hungry. Water was easier to come by; almost all of the vehicles furnished canteens for their fare's comfort. But even so, most of the passengers preferred to get out and stretch their legs and drink from banks of mountain streams whenever the drivers made watering stops for their thirsty teams. Such stops were invaluable barometers of each passenger's western "savvy": If a man drank upstream from where the draft animals were watering it indicated he was knowledgeable and wise to the country; however, if he drank downstream it was a sure sign that he was a tenderfoot!

A big problem of early day stage lines was the shortage of good teams for pulling their vehicles. Often in today's western movies the viewer will see a handsome Concord coach career through the dusty streets of some little town, drawn by six beautifully matched sorrels with blazed faces, flaxen manes and tails, and four white stockings each. But, with few exceptions, that wasn't the way it was! The demand for horses and mules of any sort was so great and the supply so short that the stage lines grabbed what they could get. Many old photos of the period show horses and mules of uneven sizes hitched side by side. In all matters involving animals, harness and other equipment, the struggling stage lines made the best of what they could find.

True, most early California stage lines had to travel roads that were extremely rough and often impassable, creature comforts of the passengers were almost non-existent, draft animals were generally ill-matched, scrawny, or "green-broke" to harness, but the greatest drawback of all was probably the lack of suitable stagecoaches. Since many of the newly formed lines were one-man, one-vehicle operations, the scarcity of coaches (and lack of money with which to buy them) forced such operators to use flatbed wagons, light spring rigs or any other four-wheeled vehicle that would serve the purpose. Some enterprising operators were thoughtful enough to install rough benches and sun awnings for comfort. One can imagine the feelings of the passenger who paid his hard-earned money for such dubious comforts. About all that could be said for the very first of the early day stage lines was that "it beat walking." Sometimes even that wasn't true!

For many years stages had been used for transportation and express in most parts of the civilized world. Though the railroads had come into their own along the Atlantic seaboard and through most of the eastern states, stage lines were operating in those same areas at greater profits than ever before. Actually, the two complemented each other, the stage lines serving sparsely settled areas where it was unprofitable for railroads to lay track, while the giant steam monsters accomodated the huge shipments of passengers and freight that fleets of stagecoaches could not have handled.

With the news of James Marshall's startling discovery, the attention of many eastern stage lines was riveted to the drama unfolding three thousand miles westward. But the general consensus of opinion was that it was far too big a gamble to rush stages, teams and personnel into an area where practically the only roads were faint mule trails that connected the Spanish missions. Besides, who knew whether or not the gold strike was real? Or how long it would last?

Nevertheless, some enterprising speculators decided to take some gambles; from France and other parts of

Europe came several old stagecoaches. Quickly they were bought up and pressed into service; just as quickly it became apparent that they were not suited to their new environment. Designed for the specific needs of countries long-settled and road-wise, the lumbering, ornate coaches were too top-heavy and dangerous for use in the Mother-lode country.

June 25, 1850, marked the beginning of a new era . . . A ship newly arrived from Boston by way of Cape Horn docked in San Francisco's harbor. A few hours later a majestic four-wheeled stagecoach rolled down Montgomery Street, its bright yellow spokes spinning and gleaming in the California sunshine while the erect "whip" maneuvered the ribbons of six superbly matched bays. Wide-eyed San Franciscans nodded approvingly as they noted the ornate gold trim and magnificient craftsmanship of the big stage.

The Concord had arrived!

The handsome coach derived its name from the capital city of New Hampshire where it was manufactured. For many years Abbott and Downing had been building fine carriages and coaches on South Street in Concord. Now, overnight, there developed a need for their fine product that would keep their shops busy for many years. The Concord was everything that could be desired in performance, handling and serviceability along the western frontier. It was almost as though Abbott and Downing had been waiting in the wings for the proper moment to introduce their brainchild to a fully approving audience comprising the entire western frontier!

The founder of the company was Lewis Downing who had come to the city of Concord in 1813. Later he was joined by J. Stephen Abbott, noted for his ability to expedite the construction of the various coaches and carriages made by the firm. Together Abbott and Downing made quite a team. Perfectionists, they handpicked every one of the 300 craftsmen who worked in their four-acre factory, making sure each understood his assigned task.

Work at the factory started early each day and didn't stop until 9 P.M. when the final bell rang to end the twelve-to-fourteen hour day.

When the two founders started designing the Concord they were greatly influenced by the lines of the conventional English mail coach. Carefully they studied it, making many changes to adapt it to the rough terrain of North and South America. To give their "baby" more roadability, they built it lower to the ground, thereby enabling it to take sharp curves at a higher rate of speed. To get rid of the top-heaviness found in most coaches, they built the upper part of thin, hand-laminated sheets of Basswood, carefully curving them to reduce wind-resistance and drag. Throughout the construction their precision and care in design was matched by their use of special woods and gluing processes. To illustrate how well they achieved their aims, one of their Concords "went down" with the ship that was bearing it from Boston to San Francisco. Approximately thirty days later the stagecoach was rescued from its watery grave and put into service. Records bear out the fact that it gave great service for fifty years!

The spokes of each Concord were made of carefully seasoned ash and hand-fitted to the rim and hub. All work was done by hand except that required to cut the felloes; for that operation horse-powered bandsaws were used. The threading of an axle was an extremely tedious operation, requiring four men. The die was placed in a vertical position, then, slowly and carefully, a man walked around the axle until the threading process was completed. The front wheels of the Concord stood three feet high while the rear measured a full five feet. Its approximate weight, unloaded, was about twenty-five hundred pounds.

Most of the Concords had upholstered seats inside to accommodate nine passengers. Three faced forward, three faced to the rear and a seat in the center held three more. In addition, at least another half-dozen passengers could find space atop the coach, riding behind the driver and his shotgun guard. But the Concord was somewhat expandable. An article from the *Butte Record* of Oroville, California, in the year 1858 read: "A stage from Shasta passed through town yesterday, about one o'clock, with an enormous load. The coach was of the biggest size. We counted thirty-five persons on and inside of it, besides the driver and one Chinaman."

The driver's box was constructed to hold the driver and two other persons, if necessary. Beneath it was an area carefully designed to store the "strong-box" or other valuables. In later years the well-known little green box of Wells Fargo was often bolted to the coach, making it harder for bandits to reach. At the rear of the coach was the "boot," usually a leather-covered, triangular rack for the purpose of carrying letters, packages and other baggage.

One of the greatest features of the Concord was its suspension system. Instead of using iron springs, such as those employed by spring wagons and other vehicles, the Concord rode suspended on leather thoroughbraces. These wide rawhide straps were attached to the front and rear axles by means of C-shaped braces and were replaced easily whenever needed. The use of this particular system did away with much of the up-and-down jarring effect, causing the oval-shaped body to rock gently as it traveled. Mark Twain, in *Roughing It,* wrote of a journey he had made in a Concord, describing the coach as a "cradle on wheels."

John Burgum and his son, Edgar, hand-decorated every stage that was made in the old Concord shop. The gold striping, scroll work, and lettering were pridefully done and truly a work of art. On the door panels there might be an oil painting of Mount Washington and another might show New England's well-known Old Man of the Mountain.

The cost of an average Concord, delivered in California, was between twelve and fifteen hundred dollars.

The records are hazy regarding how many Concords were sold to Wells Fargo and the other stage lines of

California. But it is known that in 1867 Wells Fargo bought forty coaches, the largest single order in Abbott and Downing's history. While visiting the World's Fair in New York in the year 1939, Edgar Burgum found a coach bearing the serial number 274. "That was just the beginning," he said, of the total number of Concord coaches built. And, bearing out his statement, the pages of western Americana is filled with countless stories of the great Concords, the vehicle destined to transport the pioneers of the western frontier for over half a century!

The Concord had a lowly cousin called the mudwagon. Built more cheaply, lower to the ground, with canvas side-curtains and weighing much less, the mudwagon also used the thoroughbrace suspension system. With its extremely low center of gravity the mudwagon was very practical for use in the mountain areas and during rainy seasons.

Traveling by coach was often quite eventful in the early days of the West . . . A traveler describes a typical departure from a Stockton stage depot in the year 1852:

> The driver climbed to his seat; then the team began to make its appearance; each animal securely held by two men; two animals were secured to the wagon tongue; six more were then hitched up three abreast. The lines were passed to the driver. While all this was going on, it became apparent to the passengers that a band of wild mustangs were being harnessed to speed us on our way, which they faithfully did. A line of men stood at each side of the team until the last tug was secured and the last ribbon passed up to the driver. I then heard him call out, "let go!" The stage appeared to leap from the ground and cleave through the air like a railroad train . . . On reaching the foot of the mountains the passengers all alighted and walked. It would have been unsafe to have walked behind or on either side, as the team scratched their way up that fearful grade; the air appeared thick with stones flying through the air like a hailstorm.

Stage depots were exciting places each morning as the various stages prepared to start out on their journeys. In Sacramento the coaches and their four-ups and six-ups lined an entire block waiting while baggagemen bustled back and forth with freight, agents shouted through hand-held megaphones announcing departures, and runners attempted to hustle passengers aboard the right vehicle. And, just as still happens in the present age, baggage was sometimes lost and shipped east, west, or in some other unknown direction.

All in all, it was a very intriguing sight for the local citizenry; and you can bet that most checker and domino games, wittlin' and arguin' and other activities of the town-square set ceased until "after the stage runs."

As far as the actual journeys were concerned, what some regarded as sheer torture were pleasant outings to others as per the following commentary from Hutching's *California Magazine* for 1860:

> The coach inside contained seven. Outside, three unhappy gentlemen had the pleasure of dangling their legs over the boot, receiving the full benefit of the dust. Seven or eight others hung theirs over the sides, while I with several others fixed ourselves turk

fashion upon the top. Railroads and steamboats are all very well if a person wants to be rushed through on business—but for comfort and pleasure give me the old coach, when the day is fine, and the road hard, when the teams at the changes come up fresh, and the horses go to their collars with a will and make the bounding stage rattle on the solid ground—when the boxes talk, and the passengers converse, and the driver feels in a jolly good humor—oh, then give me the old stage coach; and for music, the crack! crack! of the merry lash, and the whir-r-r-r-l-l-l-l of the flying wheels.

But the Rev. Mr. Sessions had a different opinion of his stage ride. Upon reaching the goldcamp known as Auburn in August of '55, the elderly gentleman had this experience:

> . . . on starting, a large rough man got my seat on the outside of the stage; though the agent at Sacramento and here told him it was pledged to me as an old man and an invalid; and he refused to get off unless taken off by force. It was of no use for me to try to get my right; for the passengers were all of the same sort—miners armed with revolvers and knives, and would have taken his part; and the agent of the Stage Co. dared not interfere. So I had to get inside, where the heat and dust were awful. I never rode more uncomfortably than I did from that time till 11 o'clock at night.

One afternoon a Concord coach was descending a narrow, winding mountain trail when it met a wagon. The stage driver, a man named Colby, ordered all of his passengers to get out of the coach. When they had complied he started to ease the coach by the side of the wagon. Suddenly the teams panicked and plunged over the side of the mountainside. In desperation Colby leaped for his life. Quickly the passengers rushed to the edge of the three hundred foot cliff, fully expecting to see the coach, horses and driver far below. But luckily the coach had caught on a tree thirty feet below, knocking its front undercarriage off. The sturdy coach was undamaged, otherwise. The frightened teams, still harnessed and dragging the front underpinning, ran all the way to the next stage stop.

On another occasion a coach rolled down a mountainside, spilling its passengers and freight. When the dust had settled the startled passengers picked themselves up, stretched to check for possible injuries. Finding themselves unhurt, they reloaded their baggage and continued their journey. One more feather in the cap of the firm of Abbott and Downing who built their vehicles so safely and sturdily!

British travelers were not very happy with stagecoaching in the west. Sir Henry Huntley made a journey from Sacramento to Hangtown and was quite put out by the lack of class division aboard the stages. Obviously accustomed to the deference normally accorded his title, the Britisher wrote: "The passenger coolly gets into the vehicle, and placing himself between two others, sits down, and relies upon his own weight making the other two sufficiently uncomfortable, to aid him in establishing himself between them." Sir Henry was also displeased by his fellow-passenger's excessive use of tobacco and foul language.

Another Englishman, Frank Marryat, wrote a book, *Mountains and Molehills,* about his stagecoach experiences. He describes some of his fellow-passengers during a trip to Sonora in 1851, one of them a Canadian woman who traveled under the protection of an ill-looking dog, a "quarrelsome and bumptious" Yankee armed with a revolver, and two or three miners who "squirted their juice at passing objects on the road with astonishing accuracy." Marryat said of the roads traveled by his stage: "no one knows what a wagon will undergo until he has mastered the California trails and gulches."

Marryat gave a vivid description of the monotonous bills of fare at the various way stations where stops were made to change teams. He said that inevitably they "consisted of a tough beefsteak, boiled potatoes, stewed beans, a nasty compound of dried apples, and a JUG OF MOLASSES." But the Englishman concluded that to a hungry passenger this food must have been palatable, because he would "sit down at the summons of a bell . . . and, with the point of his knife . . . taste of the various condiments . . . pile them on his plate, demolish them with a relish, and depart on his way in peace."

Hinton R. Helper, a traveler on the Stockton-Sonora route, said his stage passed over a "somewhat elevated plain," the same being "entirely destitute of trees and other vegetable products," presented a "most dreary and uninviting prospect." After lunch, Hinton said, the road was very winding as it advanced over "rocky glades, hills and gullies," and the passengers were "jarred and shaken without mercy." Helper was very negative in his treatment of Sonora's hotel accomodations: "The best hotel in the place is a one-story structure, built of unhewn saplings, covered with canvas and floored with dirt. It consists of one undivided room, in which the tables, berths and benches are all arranged. Here we sleep, eat and drink. Four or five tiers of berths or bunks, one directly above another, are built against the walls of the cabin . . . The bedding is composed of a small straw mattress about two foot wide, an uncased pillow . . . and a single blanket."

In her book, *Incidents on Land & Water or, Four years on the Pacific Coast*, Mrs. D.B. Bates described one incident she had witnessed at Marysville:

> One night about eleven o'clock, a lady came into the hotel looking more dead than alive. She was leading a little girl, of about seven years of age, who was in the same plight as her mother. They were both covered with bruises, scratches, and blood, with their garments soiled and torn. They were coming from Bidwell's Bar, a place about forty miles from Marysville, in a stage-coach, in which were nine Chinamen.

The coach was all closed, as it was rather cool in the mountains in the evening. All at once, they found themselves turning somersaults. The coach was overturned down a steep bank. All the Chinamen, with their long cues reaching to their heels, were rolling and tumbling about in the most ungraceful manner imaginable. They were vociferating at the top of their voices in a language which, if spoke calmly and with the greatest mellifluence, is harsh and disagreeable in the extreme. "And," said she, the woman in the hotel at Marysville, "such a horrid din of voices as rang in my ears, it was scarcely possible to conceive of; which, together with the freight, was almost sufficient to deprive me of my reason." The driver was seriously hurt, and so were some of the horses; but the inside passengers escaped without having any limbs broken, but their "cues" were awfully disarranged.

Such was stagecoach travel in the Motherlode's early days as recorded by a few writers who were there. But the situation was changing. In his message to the California State Legislature on January 5, 1855, Governor John Bigler stated: "Inland travel between all the principle parts of the state by means of stages, has . . . been rendered expeditious and comfortable. Indeed, California today can boast of stage and coach conveyance equal, if not superior, to any of her sister states."

Slowly but surely the overall picture was changing; slowly but surely the newcomers were pushing back the edges of the frontier, blasting, scraping and filling, corduroying and planking, building roads that would allow the passage of humanity and goods so vital to the development of the American West!

CHAPTER
IV

BLACK
BART

"Yah!" Big John Shine yelled at the top of his leathery lungs as he flicked the checklines, urging the four-up into the beginning of the long climb near Funk's Hill. Startled, the lathered animals lunged forward, tightening the traces, hooves digging deeper into the gravel as they struggled to pull the huge stagecoach with its human cargo and the Wells Fargo strongbox up the steep, narrow grade.

The afternoon sun beat down upon the thirsty arriero as he jounced about on the rough seat. He liked this Sonora-Milton run and was looking forward to stopping at Milton, Calaveras County, California. Yeah, it was a good place to spend the night! Soon the two teams would be swigging long and deep at the livery stable's trough, then rubbed down real good and grained. And while that was happening Big John would be wetting his whistle and enjoying the fine feed over at the hotel. Musing, he clucked at the teams, urging them into a little trot.

Suddenly John Shine stomped at the brake lever on the right side of the box. Bracing himself against the floorboards of the box, he yanked frantically at the ribbons, fighting to bring the two tons of steel, wood and humanity to a halt! Inside the ornate coach startled yells and screams rang out as his passengers were thrown about like rag dolls. At the last second the locked wheels of the big Concord slid to a stop just inches away from the cliff's edge. Big John Shine mopped his sweaty brow with the back of a big calloused paw and stared down at the dizzy precipice. That had been close, too close!

Angry voices sounded from within the coach. Some of the more irate passengers began to curse the man atop the box for his handling of the ribbons, blaming him for bumped heads, ruffled tempers and for the hovering dust making it almost impossible for them to breathe!

But Big John Shine was staring wide-eyed, ignoring his disgruntled fares . . . Standing just fifteen feet in front of the spooked-up leaders was the most grotesque, most fear-inspiring sight the veteran driver had ever seen! Wearing a hood improvised from a faded flour sack with rough-cut eyeholes, black baggy trousers hidden partially by a soiled linen duster and with shoes covered by heavy socks (obviously worn to eliminate leaving footprints) the ghastly spectre stared up at the Wells Fargo driver from behind the twin barrels of a deadly sawed-off shotgun!

"Please . . . throw down the box!" The road agent's courteous words of request rang deep and hollow upon the mountain air, muffled slightly by the hood he was wearing.

Warily Big John Shine studied the situation. For the past several years the local stage runs had been so routine and uneventful that often as not no guard was aboard —such was the situation today. He eyed the bandit, wondering if it would be possible to stampede the jittery teams and run the stagecoach over the outlaw before he could pull the trigger.

As if reading his thoughts the hooded man "eared back" the remaining hammer of the "shoot-twice." Turning his head slightly, the bandit spoke to some unseen figure in the dense brush at the side of the trail. "All right, men. If he so much as makes a foolish move or goes for a gun, blast him off the box!"

The cold words rang across the trail like a death knell! A shiver coursed up the driver's spine as he stared past the yawning gun barrels and into the eerie hooded eyes! At that moment there was no doubt in John Shine's mind that the grotesquely garbed bandit would pull the trigger if he had to! And furthermore, the man was not alone! Slowly and carefully Big John scanned the area. There! Over on top of that big rock he could see the tip of a rifle barrel! And there . . . there was another! Three, four, five, six . . . why, counting the hooded outlaw, there were at least seven armed men, all with guns aimed at the stage!

Big John Shine had lots of savvy. Any fool could see that the big Concord coach and its occupants would be riddled by the first volley should the driver or any of the passengers make a rash move. Slowly he edged around in his seat. He rapped on the top of the coach to get attention. With all the authority he could muster, he barked a warning. "Hey! Hear me and hear me good! We're surrounded by seven armed men with guns pointed at this stage! If you value your lives, sit back, shut up, and don't make any foolish moves!"

The low muttering from within the coach ceased instantly as the passengers digested his words and decided to heed the advice.

The hooded man had been watching. Now he nodded in approval, "You made good sense!" He made a slight gesture with the sawed-off. "All right, now. Like I said before, throw down the box!"

The time for guessing games was over. Hurriedly Big John moved to comply. Grunting and straining with the effort, he wrestled the green wooden box from beneath his seat and tossed it to the ground.

Nonchalantly, the hooded bandit transferred the shotgun to the crook of his left arm and called out to the men hidden in the brush, "Now, you men look right sharp while I open the box and see what we've got here!"

Reaching inside his duster, the outlaw produced a small hand-ax. Vigorously he attacked the strongbox. Two minutes later it was open, revealing several bags of gold coins and some express packages. Cooly he stuffed the booty into his various pockets and, as if satisfied with the amount and quality of the strongbox's contents, nodded his head, creating an eerie effect as the hood moved back and forth.

Turning, he stalked ceremoniously to the coach and peered in. For a long moment his hooded eyes scanned the subdued passengers. Suddenly his right hand flicked to his forehead in a gesture of salute. Then, with the air of a military commander on a mission of importance, he turned to Big John Shine. "All right, driver. You may drive on. But I must warn you that my associates and I will stay here for a little while. So, should you or any of your passengers . . ."

But the rest of the highwayman's words were cut off as the heavy coach lurched forward. With mixed emotions of fear, frustration and anger, Big John Shine put his teams into a dead run. Uphill and down, hooves churning, manes and tails flying in the wind, the sweat-covered animals broke all records as they raced toward Milton and the nearest law enforcement agencies.

The giant golden ball of sun was teetering upon the edge of the western horizon as the speeding coach roared into the little mining village. Belatedly the armed male passengers were shooting from the Concord's windows, alerting the startled citizenry that violence had returned to Calaveras County!

Big John braked his vehicle to a sliding halt in front of the sheriff's office. The dust had not settled before the big coach was hemmed in by noisy, excited citizens, each shouting and clamoring to learn the reasons for the stage's breakneck speed and gunshots. Hearing the commotion, the sheriff, a veteran of the gold country, emerged from a nearby store and took command. Gravely he listened as Big John gave his account of the holdup. From time to time the driver was interrupted as his passengers broke in excitedly to add their comments.

The reports of the driver and passengers all agreed that the hooded bandit had not worked alone, there had been many gun barrels leveled at the coach. When John Shine returned to the site of the hold-up he was startled to find the "guns" still in position and aimed at the spot where the coach had halted! They were only sticks, obviously whittled and placed to look like rifle and shotgun barrels.

In time, Monday, July 26, 1975 became a day that Wells Fargo would not forget, because events to come proved it to be the debut of the most extraordinary stagecoach robber the old West would ever know . . . the entrance into crime of Black Bart, P08—the poet of the highwaymen!

Five months passed with no further news or action by the phantom bandit . . . Then, on December 28, the stage making the San Juan-Marysville run was stopped by the same grotesquely garbed robber. The second holdup was a repeat of the first. The bandit was extremely courteous, calm and businesslike, the Wells Fargo treasury was lighter by several hundred dollars when the gun party was over, and the hastily organized posse could find no clues, tracks, or trail of any kind!

The newspapers devoted much space to the holdup, relating how one slightly built outlaw had robbed the stage and walked away with pockets bulging with Wells Fargo valuables, leaving no trail of any kind. The story was read and retold many times, gaining something with each telling. Overnight the hooded bandit became the center of discussion around every cracker barrel, barber shop, and gathering place throughout the gold country!

The Yreka-Roseburg stage, operating near the Oregon state line, was his target five months later. Again the hooded outlaw followed his regular pattern during the robbery. And when a woman passenger panicked and handed him her purse, he soothed her fears and gallantly handed it back, saying, "Thank you, madam, but I don't need your money. I only want Wells Fargo's!"

The cavalierish incident made the headlines everywhere! Reams of copy were written about the courteous, soft-spoken gold country bandit. And, since he had never taken money from passengers or hurt anyone, many of the stories had a tendency to romanticize the mysterious figure who was jousting with one of the West's most dynamic business enterprises.

When informed of the hooded bandit's statement about "wanting only Wells Fargo's money," Lloyd Tevis, president of the company, immediately alerted his general superintendent, John J. Valentine and other top-level executives. The lights burned late at the corner of California and Montgomery Streets that night! And when the planning session was ended James Hume, the very capable and well-liked Chief of Wells Fargo detectives had been assigned to handle the case and bring the phantom bandit to justice. Hume let no grass grow under his feet. Hurriedly he engaged Harry Morse, a very reputable private detective from San Francisco to assist himself and Johnny Thacker, another longtime Wells Fargo lawman. The gauntlet had been thrown and Wells Fargo was taking up the battle!

For the next twelve months the stages plied their runs with no trouble from the unpredictable highwayman. And then, on August 3, 1877, he struck for the fourth time. The Point Arenas coach, bound for Duncan Mills, was stopped near Fort Ross and liberated of $300 in gold coin and a negotiable check. But this time the canny holdup artist added a unique touch. When the posse rode up to the holdup site they found the following poem (written on a Wells Fargo waybill) in the rifled strongbox:

I've labored long and hard for bread
For honor and for riches,

But on my corns too long you've tread,
You fine-haired sons of bitches.

Each of the four lines of poetry was written by hand, and in a different script. The waggish poem bore the signature: Black Bart the P08. As usual, the slight bandit walked away on foot. And, as usual, the trail he left behind was as cold as a loose woman's heart! But for all who were following the outlaw's career his latest holdup was a milestone . . . At last the phantom bandit had a name!

The poem left at the holdup led many people to believe that the stagecoach robber was a longtime enemy of Wells Fargo. With that thought in mind Jim Hume and his men started examining the company's files, looking for information regarding disgruntled passengers or freight customers who might fit the known description of the robber. But once again their quest proved to be fruitless!

Meanwhile rumors spread over the gold country . . . Black Bart had been seen here, had eaten with a rancher and his family there, and so on. Tirelessly Hume and his men investigated each report, but all were eventually proven false, born of idle speculation and gossip.

For over a year Hume and his men had been working on the case without a breakthrough. Now the Wells Fargo chief of detectives and his staff went over all the countless bits of information they had compiled, noting the many similarities:

(1) The robber had arrived at and left each holdup on foot.
(2) He always carried the same articles on his clothing or in an old valise. They were: a sawed-off shotgun, small hand-axe, crowbar, and a sledge hammer.
(3) He had never yet robbed a passenger.
(4) He had worn the flour sack hood during each holdup.
(5) He had never fired his shotgun.
(6) He had always been courteous and had a good sense of humor.

(7) A man of about 50 or more had been seen in the vicinity of each holdup and had often partaken of food (as was the custom in those days) at nearby ranches and homes. He was described by his various hosts as soft-spoken, educated, very likeable and claimed to have seen service as a Captain of Illinois Infantry Volunteers during the Civil War. When the suggestion had been raised that he was the infamous Black Bart, all the people contacted declared it was impossible, that he was too nice and gentlemanly.

Jim Hume had new "flyers" printed with all the information that had accumulated concerning the phantom highwayman. The circulars also listed the amount of reward being offered by Wells Fargo and the United States government. Hoping to get a break in the case, the Wells Fargo man sent copies of the handbills to every law agency, post office and gathering place throughout the West. In the meantime orders went out to have more armed guards on the stage runs. Step-by-step Jim Hume and Wells Fargo were preparing the defense that would someday result in the apprehension of their enemy.

As if sensing the gathering of forces by his enemy, Black Bart stayed away from the bandit trail until July 24, 1878. One morning as the Quincy-Oroville stage approached Berry Creek, the driver noticed a tall, middle-aged man squatting by the roadside, busily writing with pen and paper. The driver waved at the man and continued his run, thinking no more about the incident until the following morning. As the stage reached the same spot where he had seen the man on the previous day, a hooded figure stepped out into the road with a levelled shotgun. Quickly he liberated $379 in gold coin from the strongbox, plus a gold watch and a small amount of mail. Within an hour a posse descended upon the scene. They found the second verse written by the poet of the badlands. Bearing the signature of Black Bart, it read:

here I lay me down to Sleep
to wait the coming morrow
perhaps Success perhaps defeat
And everlasting Sorrow
I've labored long and hard for bred·
for honor and for riches
But on my corns too long you've tred
you fine haired sons of bitches
let come what will I'll try it on
my condition can't be worse
and if there's money in that Box
Tis munny in my purse

Like the first poem, each line was written in a different type of script.

Again the hue and cry arose and Hume and his men were here and there, tracking down countless rumors. Wells Fargo added more money to the reward upon the outlaw's head but there were no takers. Again the trail grew cold.

And then for some unknown reason, the bandit stepped up his assault upon the stage lines. Five months later he struck again. Then two months after that holdup he confounded his pursuers by robbing one stage one day and walking thirty-five miles over rough country to hold up another Wells Fargo coach the following afternoon!

Black Bart's twenty-third holdup occurred July 13, 1882. His target was the stage from Laporte to Oroville. For the first time during his seven years of banditry he met resistance. Stepping out from the side of the trail he waved his shotgun and ordered the box to be thrown down. For a moment the driver and the shotgun guard eyed the strangely garbed figure. Suddenly the man riding shotgun, George W. Hackett, raised his rifle and fired at the bandit. The hooded figure tumbled backwards into the nearby brush! Hackett and the driver, George Helms, leaped down from the box and with weapons ready, cautiously stalked the outlaw. But the dense brush enabled the holdup artist to make his getaway! Searching the ground where he had fallen the men found his hat. Excitedly they stared at the bullet hole through the crown of the derby. Turning the hat over they saw the fresh blood stains . . . They had wounded Black Bart!

Wells Fargo was greatly excited! Perhaps the bandit's injuries would prevent him from returning to the outlaw trail!

But time proved them to be premature in their rejoicing . . . Within the next several months there were more holdups by the hooded man, four, to be exact. Again Hume had flyers circulated throughout the country, hoping that the reward being offered for the outlaw would result in his capture. But still there were no takers. Wearily James Hume and his men added up the score. Since that black date of July 26, 1875, the notorious bandit had robbed twenty-seven Wells Fargo stagecoaches and stolen thousands of dollars, and still he was as free as a bird, his identity unknown!

Black Bart's fame and reputation had spread around the world. It was only natural that his success would lead others to imitate him. Soon "Bill Smith" was holding up the stages travelling through the Sierras while Dick Fellows was working the coast road leading south from San Francisco.

Saturday, November 3, 1883, Black Bart's luck ran out . . . Ironically it happened on the Milton-Sonora run, the very same run that he had held-up during his first robbery eight years before!

Reason McConnell drove the big stage out of Sonora at four o'clock in the morning. In his strongbox was approximately $500 in gold coin, $4,100 in amalgam and a small quantity of gold dust. Due to another of Wells Fargo's precautions, the strongbox was bolted to the floor beneath the driver's seat. The change had been initiated to make it harder for a holdup man to get the box open.

Reaching Reynold's Ferry, the driver pulled up his empty stage to make the usual stop at a small hotel run by "Grandma" Rolleri. Waiting outside the building was her young son, Jimmy. The youth boarded the stage, planning to ride as far as Copperopolis where he intended to hunt for deer. McConnell and his passenger rode along, visiting and discussing local happenings, little dreaming of things to come!

As the stage started to climb a long hilly grade the youth got off, saying he would hunt along the trail and rejoin the stage when it reached the other side of the hill. A moment later the boy was gone from view, swallowed up by the thick underbrush.

Reason McConnell concentrated on his driving, easing the four-up along the steep climb. Suddenly, as he neared the crest of the hill, a hooded figure, familiar to many stage drivers, stepped out of the dense manzanita along the trail. His sawed-off shotgun tilted upward, covering the stage driver.

"All right, driver. Get down from there so that I can get to the box!"

The bandit's remark triggered the stage driver's curiosity. How had he known that the box would be bolted down?

Once again the bandit spoke, "I've told you once. Get down from that box!" The bandit's tone was sharper this time.

Defiantly the driver replied, "You've got my team all spooked up. The brakes aren't very good and if I'm not careful the team could run away while I'm gettin' down!"

"The stage couldn't roll if you put some rocks behind the wheels."

"Yeah. But I'm up here tryin' to hold 'em. You're down there. Why don't you do it?"

The bandit was irritated. For a moment he stared, then he moved to the side of the trail and picked up some rocks. Carefully he placed rocks behind each wheel. "All right, they're scotched. Now, unhitch your teams and drive 'em down the road a few yards. Not too far, and remember I'll be watching you while I'm up there opening the box."

Quickly McConnell did as ordered. He was standing a

63

few yards away when he heard a slight rustling in the nearby brush. Turning, the driver saw young Jimmy Rolleri approaching, his rifle slung over his shoulder. Frantically McConnell signalled the boy, trying to get his attention. The youth was just a few feet away when he saw the hooded bandit and realized what was happening. Quickly he threw his rifle to his shoulder and triggered a shot. He missed and fired again as the outlaw dived from the driver's seat. Reason McConnell grabbed the gun from the boy's hands. He sighted at the running man for a brief instant and pulled the trigger.

With the roar of the gun the outlaw went sprawling to the ground, dropping some papers he was carrying. McConnell ran toward the spot, ready to fire again if he had the chance. And then the bandit was up and running, quickly disappearing in the thick vegetation.

McConnell and young Jimmy Rolleri searched the area, finding the papers they had seen the bandit drop. The papers were stained with fresh blood! McConnell had hit him!

Hurriedly they rehitched the four-up and sped into Copperopolis. They reported the holdup to Sheriff B.K. Thorn, and in turn he sent a message notifying the Wells Fargo organization in San Francisco.

The sheriff and his posse raced to the holdup site. They could find no trail leading away from the scene but their investigation turned up several articles belonging to the bandit. In his hurry to escape the deadly marksmanship of Reason McConnell Black Bart had left behind a belt, razor, two empty flour sacks, a magnifying glass used to examine mining samples, a leather case designed to carry field glasses, three soiled shirt cuffs, and a handkerchief filled with buckshot. The posse also found two paper bags filled with sugar and crackers behind a rock where the man had eaten while waiting for the stage.

The sheriff and his men swarmed over the nearby countryside, questioning everyone they met. Two men reported seeing a man who fit the general description (as far as size and age were concerned) of the bandit. At nearby Angel's Camp a local storekeeper told the posse that a man resembling the outlaw had bought food there a few days before. This led the sheriff and his men to believe that the outlaw had stayed in the vicinity a few days while checking the stage schedule and planning his escape route.

Sheriff B.K. Thorn was a thorough man ... While awaiting the arrival of the Wells Fargo detectives he examined the articles the outlaw had left behind. At last he unwrapped the handkerchief and laid the buckshot to one side. He stared for a few moments. Suddenly he called out, "Hey! I think we've got something!"

Excitedly the others gathered.

Thorn pointed at the handkerchief. On one corner of the piece of soiled linen was printed FX07. It was a laundry mark!

Jim Hume and his men were elated to learn of the sheriff's discovery. Carefully they analyzed its meaning. None of the small towns in the area used such a modern day device as a laundry mark. (To be truthful, most of the small towns did not have laundries. They were considered extremely fortunate if they had a laundress!) Therefore Hume decided to search in San Francisco first, hoping that some clue would turn up there. If not, then they would search all the other larger towns.

Hume assigned Harry Morse to check out all of San Francisco's laundries. A check at the business license department revealed that there were 91 laundries within the city. Doggedly Morse bowed his neck and plunged into his task!

Day in and day out the weary detective continued his quest ... On the eighth day he hit paydirt!

Thomas C. Ware, owner of a laundry located at 316 Bush Avenue, eyed the small piece of linen and nodded his head. "Yessir, that's our mark."

After seven years of searching for some clue that would lead to unmasking Black Bart's identity Harry Morse could hardly hide his excitement! "Well, Mr. Ware, would your records give us the name of the man you did this laundry for?"

Thomas Ware stepped to a dusty filing cabinet in the corner of his office. He thumbed through a ledger for a moment. "Yep, here it is. Hey, we did that for ol' Charley. Uh, his full name is Charles E. Bolton. He's a retired mining engineer who comes to San Francisco every once in a while. Nice fellow. And usually when he's in town he hangs out here with us and visits. Charley's a right good talker. Good to have around."

"Mr. Ware, do your records show when you did this?"

"Oh, yes. The first time was back in July of this year. Then we did this same handkerchief again for ol' Charley on Saturday, August 11."

"One last thing, Mr. Ware. Do your records show where we can contact Mr. Bolton?"

Suddenly the man stared at Harry Morse, his brow wrinkling. "By the way, do you mind telling me what this is all about? I wouldn't want to butt in on Charley's business and make him mad at me for talking too much."

Harry Morse was not ready to tell the man any more than he had to. There were still too many loose ends in the case and if Ware told the suspect about Morse's questions the man might flee the area. He dropped his voice confidentially and winked at the man. "Well, this has to stay just between the two of us for the present. As you know, Mr. Bolton is a mining man and has some claims that some friends of mine would like to buy. Fact is, they would pay a pretty penny for them. Mr. Bolton had dropped this handkerchief and it was the only way we knew to get in touch with him. But, if you were to tell Mr. Bolton you might upset the applecart." Morse smiled at the man, exuding an air of camaraderie.

Thomas Ware smiled. He liked this man. And it looked like ol' Charley might really profit from this visit. "Mr. Morse, I understand. And I'm glad to help ol' Charley any way I can. Let's see. Charley's over at the Webb House in room 200. Been there a couple of days. The Webb House is easy to find, over on 2nd street."

Hardly believing his good fortune Harry Morse hurried to the nearest police headquarters and arranged for policemen to be posted at the Webb House around the clock, ready to apprehend the suspect when all the pieces of evidence were fitted into place.

When that had been accomplished and the policemen were in place, Morse returned to see Thomas Ware. Noting the man's surprise at his early return, the detective explained. "Mr. Ware, I don't want to impose upon your good nature but it just so happened that I ran into my people and they'd like to get with Mr. Bolton as soon as possible. So would you mind walking over to the Webb with me and introducing me to Mr. Bolton?"

A moment later Ware was introducing the two men, explaining that Morse represented mining interests who were interested in claims. As the laundryman talked, Morse watched the suspect, appraising his manner and reactions. Suddenly Morse was certain the suspect was Black Bart! The man's voice, manner, physical description, all added up!

Quickly they said their goodbyes to the laundryman and the detective led the so-called "mining engineer" toward the heart of San Francisco's business district. As they walked they talked of the mining business, exchanging views on events that had happened throughout the years. A few minutes later they neared the Wells Fargo building. As Morse led the suspect into the entrance the slender man looked up at the Wells Fargo sign for an instant, then continued with no sign of suspicion. And then they were entering James Hume's office.

Hume shook hands with the stranger and asked him to be seated. Following Morse's lead, Hume asked the bogus mining expert where his properties were located. With an air of casualness the man replied "that they were in Nevada, on the California side."

A moment or so later the suspect grew reticent. He quit talking and began to nervously wipe his brow.

The two detectives saw the scars of a recent wound upon the man's hand. Hume pointed and commented, "You've hurt yourself . . . and recently. How did that happen?"

"C.E. Bolton" lost his temper. "I fell while getting off a train. Now, you've brought me down here and my patience is spent. I'm not going to answer any more questions!"

Morse turned the conversation back to the man's mining claims, temporarily creating an opportunity for Hume to leave the room and send for a policeman. A few minutes later Captain Stone of the San Francisco Police Department arrived. He was advised privately by Jim Hume what was happening. Captain Stone listened for a few moments, then, against Bolton's objections, hailed a hack and had the party driven back to the Webb House.

Going to the suspect's room, the officers began a thorough search of the quarters. Then they turned their attention to an old trunk and three valises.

The suspect was indignant. "What right do you have to search my things. Are you mistaking me for a stage robber?"

The man's actions and very words convinced the Wells Fargo men that they were on the right track. Suddenly Harry Morse straightened from the search of a valise. In his hand was another handkerchief that bore the same laundry mark as the one dropped by Black Bart at his last stage robbery. A moment later a letter written in the same hand and script as the poetry of Black Bart was found in another valise.

Captain Stone was convinced! He eyed the suspect. "You're under arrest. Let's go to headquarters!"

The suspect smiled, "Under arrest? What for?"

Jim Hume answered. "Because you're Black Bart!"

The prisoner was escorted to jail. Upon being booked he told the desk sergeant that his name was T.Z. Spalding.

Jim Hume and Morse watched as the steel doors closed behind the man. As they walked through the night they felt that the end of the chase was near. They hurried back to the Wells Fargo Building and discussed ways to strengthen their case.

The following morning the prisoner was asked to try on the derby dropped by Black Bart at his last stage holdup. To no one's surprise, it fitted perfectly.

The prisoner chuckled. "Hey, this hat fits me very well. May I ask, would you sell it to me?"

Hours and hours of questioning followed. But in spite of every bit of evidence and logic presented by the officers, the man continued to deny his guilt.

Hoping to get a confession, the prisoner was driven to Milton where he was brought face to face with Reason E. McConnell, the driver who had aborted Black Bart's last holdup.

McConnell stared at the suspect. "Well, I can't be certain, because the man I shot was wearing a mask over his face. Can I hear him talk a little bit?"

Hume began the questioning. For a moment or so the suspect refused to talk. Then, evidently realizing that failure to speak could be construed as a sign of guilt, he began to answer the questions.

Suddenly McConnell interrupted. "That's enough. I'd know that voice anywhere. That's Black Bart!"

In spite of the identification, the prisoner continued to plead that he was innocent. He was taken to nearby San Andreas and confined overnight. The following day Jim Hume resumed his questioning. Step-by-step he reviewed the evidence, trying to show the prisoner the strength of the case that had been built against him. The suspect began to evade the questions, talking wildly and quoting from the Scriptures, reliving experiences he claimed to have had during the Civil War, and rumbling on and on about other non-related subjects.

Suddenly the prisoner grew tired of his subterfuge.

Cautiously he asked, "I'm not admitting anything. But what advantage would it be to a fellow if he admitted everything?"

Hume sensed a breakthrough in the long, tedious case. He chose his words carefully. "It would be much better for him and easier on him to admit his guilt and throw himself upon the mercy of the court. If he chose to fight the case there would be much expense, many witnesses would appear and testify how he had held guns upon them and frightened them. And a jury would be sure to rule against him and give him a much longer sentence."

"Could a confession . . . where maybe a fellow made a clean breast of everything, clear a man altogether?"

"No. But a confession would get him a much lighter sentence."

On and on the questioning continued . . .

In the wee hours of the morning the suspect looked at Jim Hume for a long moment, studying the veteran officer's face. Suddenly he nodded his head. "All right. Get your papers ready for me to sign . . . I'll confess to everything. I am Black Bart!"

And so, in the presence of Jim Hume, Harry Morse, Captain Stone and Sheriff B.K. Thorn, the prisoner recounted all the essential facts of the twenty-eight robberies he had committed over the past eight years! He told of using field glasses to study the terrain of his holdups, thereby assuring himself of a good escape route always, of learning in great detail all the pertinent facts concerning stage schedules and guard assignments, of observing which companies were shipping their valuables and the dates of such assignments. He chuckled as he told of taking the name Black Bart from a book entitled *The Case of Summerfield.*

He heaped embarrassment upon the San Francisco Police Department by telling of the time he had sat at a San Francisco dining table with several police while they discussed Black Bart and his deeds. To add salt to their wounds he described his going to a police headquarters and reporting a stolen raincoat. Naturally the San Francisco newspapers made much of those two incidents.

Following the signing of his confession, the wheels of justice turned rapidly. He pleaded guilty to only the final holdup and was sentenced to six years in San Quentin; less than three weeks after his final holdup Black Bart walked through the prison gates and became inmate No. 11046.

As might be expected, the likeable bandit became a model prisoner. During the early days of his sentence he wrote a letter to Reason E. McConnell, the driver who had shot and wounded him, causing his eventual capture. He joked about the incident and assured McConnell that he bore no hard feelings. His letter served to ease the mind of Mrs. McConnell who had worried greatly about the possibility of the prisoner seeking revenge when released from San Quentin.

Prisoner No. 11046 exhibited such a spirit of cooperation and courteous treatment to his fellow human beings that his sentence was shortened. On January 21, 1888, having served four years and two months, he walked through the towering gates of San Quentin, once again a free man.

Many newspaper reporters were waiting at the prison gates. Immediately they swarmed over the affable figure. Shouts rang out as they greeted him. "Hey, Black Bart! What'cha gonna do now? Gonna hold up any more stages?"

The slender man greeted them, smiling and shaking hands. "No, gentlemen, I'm all through with crime!"

Another reporter spoke, "Are you going to write any more poetry?"

Charles Boles shook his finger good-naturedly at the man. "Now didn't you hear me say I am through with crime?"

The newsmen roared with laughter. And the ex-stage robber's waggish joke was written up in papers everywhere.

Charles Boles grew restless after leaving prison. For a time he moved about, and then, in March of 1888, he dropped completely out of sight. Upon his disappearance rumors began to fly. Each stagecoach robbery was laid at his door, regardless of the fact that Jim Hume of Wells Fargo denied any and all such reports, pointing out that the description and methods of operation were not at all like Black Bart's! And in the year 1896 a man confessed to robbing a stage in Edgerton, Kansas, telling all who would listen that he was Black Bart! Once again the headlines were black and heavy as the rumors ran wild. To clear up the matter, Wells Fargo sent Johnny Thacker back to the midwestern state to interrogate the prisoner and see if he could be Black Bart. When Thacker returned to San Francisco he was interviewed by reporters and told them that the "prisoner in Kansas looked about as much like Black Bart as a bird's nest looks like a mile post!"

Reports drifted in that Black Bart had died, another claimed that he had tired of the western frontier and moved to Japan to live out his life. But one of the most controversial rumors that still persists to this day claims that Wells Fargo entered into an agreement with the wily outlaw; that if he would refrain from robbing their stages they would pay him a yearly stipend. The amount of this so-called compensation was conjectured to be very substantial and supposedly continued until his death. However, Wells Fargo Bank has never been able to find, among its records or elsewhere, any evidence, indication, or hint that Black Bart was ever on the company's payroll ... except what he was able to help himself to in the robberies which preceded his arrest, trial, and imprisonment.

Jim Hume, who had spent almost eight years in trying to bring the elusive bandit to the bar, wrote the final report on the matter. In his summation of the case the veteran lawman paid tribute to the outlaw's great physical stamina and endurance, chronicling the feats of walking he had performed during his twenty-eight escapes from the scenes of his crimes! He praised the man's intelligence, his ability to talk and communicate with his fellow man, and his ability to laugh at himself when the going grew tough.

He added that the man was a stickler for neatness, had friends of high repute and good morals, was always extremely polite, chaste in language, and had never been known to gamble other than on an occasional race horse or by speculating in mining stocks!

The saga of Black Bart has been told and retold . . . The magic cameras of Hollywood have duly transcribed his deeds for worldwide audiences and it is a rare week indeed that passes without some reference upon the TV screen or in the newspapers to the notorious highwayman. But one thing seems clear when the crimes of the genteel, soft-spoken man are compared to those of the current crop of dope-crazed, blood-thirsty hoodlums and law-breakers: "they just ain't makin' outlaws like they used to!"

CHAPTER
V

ROAD
AGENTS

In a sense the gold-carrying express companies were "sitting ducks" for outlaws and holdup artists in the early days. The pioneer firms set up shop in remote mining camps with little or no law enforcement, assumed responsibility for the miner's gold, then endeavored to ship it through wild, unpopulated territory to safer deposit in San Francisco. Their task was indeed Herculean, considering the rugged trails that limited transportation to horse, wagon, mule train and stage.

At first the expressmen and mail carriers were never robbed. Although the gold country had its share of brawls, killings, holdups and other crimes, there was one place where early day criminals drew the line. . . they did not steal gold. Men hung together in protecting the treasure in which they all had some sort of share.

Imagine if you will, Alexander Todd transporting $200,000 worth of gold dust from Stockton to "the bay" in an unmarked box, and without a single guard! Or the time that $1,000,000 was delivered from the gold camps to San Francisco by means of one small boat!

But as stories of such rich bonanzas trickled out of the motherlode country and circulated around the world, it was only natural that the greed of every highwayman who heard was stimulated. Gradually there was an influx of bandits and outlaws from all over the world; with their coming the immunity of the express companies and mail carriers faded away. Men from all walks of life had invaded the land in search of their fortunes; now, as lonely claims petered out or failed to produce the hoped-for bonanzas, many of the miners turned to banditry, reasoning that it would be much easier to get gold dust with a gun than with a blister-raising shovel!

Like many of their competitors of the early years, Wells Fargo did not always have guards or messengers riding with their shipments. But as the tempo of the holdups increased, the company added guards and laid down certain ground rules:

(1) Immediately after each robbery Wells Fargo reimbursed each shipper the amount of the loss.
(2) Then the company's detectives set about locating the strongbox and the bandits.

Of all the outlaws who plagued Wells Fargo, Black Bart enjoyed the greatest notoriety. Reams of publicity were written about the elusive bandit, describing his many holdups, method of operation and fantastic escapes. His 28 holdups (all of Wells Fargo shipments) were spread over 8 years. Always a loner, the poet of the highwaymen would sometimes remain inactive for a long period following one of his robberies. Then, just as Wells Fargo dared to hope that they had seen the last of him, the wily oldster would reappear along some lonely mountain trail and strike again. His one-man assault upon the coffers of Wells Fargo cost its officers, detectives, stage drivers and guards many sleepless hours before James B. Hume finally brought him to justice.

Another outlaw whose career spanned several years was Richard Barter, better known as "Rattlesnake Dick."

Born in Quebec in 1833, the son of a British army officer, the handsome, dark-haired youth was drawn to the California goldfields in 1850. He settled in the camp known as "Rattlesnake Bar" and tried his hand at prospecting for a while. Finding no "color," he finally gave up prospecting and began to run with bad companions. This association soon led to his apprehension by the local authorities on suspicion of horse stealing.

Stealing a man's horse was about as low a trick as could be pulled in the old days. Such a crime was usually punished by an informal party at the nearest tall tree; a party where the guest of honor danced on air while others looked on in satisfaction at a job well done. Young Barter was fortunate in that he was released for lack of evidence and all charges were dropped. But shortly afterwards he was arrested on a similar charge. This time he wasn't so lucky. Loudly he proclaimed to one and all that he was not guilty. But he drew a term in the state pen. After serving part of his sentence, he was released. It seems that the law had learned that, indeed, he was innocent.

•Desiring to get away from his bad companions and to make a fresh start, "Rattlesnake Dick" moved to Shasta County. But the news of his stretch in prison soon caught up with him. And, even though he had been innocent in the eyes of the law, many of the Shasta community called him a jailbird and treated him with contempt. Their rejection made the youth bitter; soon that bitterness led him into the ranks of the Reelfoot Williams outlaw band. Now he was committed to a life of outlawry. There would be no turning back.

Some historians have credited Reelfoot Williams as the first outlaw to organize a band to rob stages. According to those authorities, the debut of his gang was in the month of April, 1852, when they held up the Nevada City Coach just outside of Illinoistown and relieved it of $7,500.

Though young, and inexperienced, Richard Barter "took" to outlaw life; and when Reelfoot took off suddenly for parts unknown and a healthier climate, the youth became the band's new leader. Under his guidance the gang pulled off the $80,000 Wells Fargo mule train holdup in 1855, and the $26,000 Rhodes and Lusk Express robbery in '56.

The $80,000 stolen in the mule train holdup was never recovered. But the miners who had shipped their gold by Wells Fargo's mule train didn't lose a dime. As always, Wells Fargo promptly made good every cent of the stolen money. Since 1852, and through decade after decade the word passed down that "you can depend on Wells Fargo—no one ever lost a cent entrusted to their care." Certainly the company had a tremendous reputation for making good on any losses.

Following the Rhodes and Lusk job the bandits buried their loot and scattered in an effort to avoid capture. But a letter from one of the outlaws fell into the hands of a Wells Fargo detective. Painstakingly he unraveled the clues and finally traced the gang to a hideout near Folsom, California. There the Wells Fargo detectives and law officers closed the noose and moved in. When the shooting was over George Skinner (one of the gang) was dead, and four others, Romero, Newton, Carter and "Rattlesnake Dick" were captured.

Romero, Newton and Carter were seen behind prison bars, serving sentences. But "Rattlesnake Dick" broke out of the Auburn jail and escaped. That was the pattern of the next three years. Several times he was captured. But each time he escaped, leading many to believe the handsome outlaw bore a charmed life.

The myth of the dashing bandit's immortality was destroyed forever on the night of July 11, 1859. Shortly after sundown on that date Dick and one of his gang were spotted as they rode through Auburn. Minutes later three of the community's law officers were mounted and riding lap and tap in pursuit. A gunfight resulted when the two outlaws refused to surrender. One of the lawmen was wounded and another, George Martin, was killed in the hail of hot, flying lead. The two outlaws escaped into the

night, apparently unscratched.

But when a posse arrived upon the scene at daybreak they found sign that one of the outlaws had been seriously wounded. Warily, they followed the bloody trail. They found "Rattlesnake Dick" dead about a mile from the scene of the gunfight. He had suffered two bullets through the body and a third through his brain. The evidence led the possemen to believe that the bullet through the brain had been inflicted either by the outlaw himself, or his henchman when it became evident he had suffered his death wounds. For several years the handsome young bandit had plied his trade along the gold country trails, but at last, bullets from out of the night had ended "Rattlesnake Dick's" career!

One of the most unusual road agents was Thomas J. Hodges, alias Tom Bell. Born in the tiny village of Rome, Tennessee, he grew up on the Cumberland river and was given a good education by his parents. Graduating from medical school just as the War with Mexico erupted, he enlisted and served with honor. Discharged after the conflict ended, he was lured to the Motherlode country by James Marshall's gold strike, hoping that he could soon make his fortune. But prospecting was not his game; soon he was running out of money and drinking far too much rotgut whiskey.

He turned to petty theft to keep going but was soon caught. Convicted of grand larceny, he was sent to Angel's Island State Prison in 1855. But he had led too active a life to be content to serve his term. He fell in with five other convicts and, together, they made their escape from the prison. On the outside, a fugitive from justice who would be hunted and hounded at every turn, he decided that his only chance for survival was to form an outlaw band. This he did, using four of the convicts who had made the break from Angel's Island with him.

In an effort to confuse the law authorities, Dr. Thomas J. Hodges dropped his name. Borrowing one from another small time outlaw, he became known as Tom Bell.

The new outlaw chief was well suited for his new role in life. Possessed of a keen mind and well-educated, he was able to out-think his followers and keep them under control. To his credit, in the early days of his outlaw career he tried hard to prevent any bloodshed or killing. His policy was quite daring and extremely radical, since most of the outlaws of that time cared little for human life.

As time passed Tom Bell hardened, developed an air for showmanship, and began to swagger and show-off. He would sometimes enter a saloon and carouse for a few days. During such escapades he would brag about who he was and how he and his gang were making fools of the law. As a result of such carryings-on, he was shot at several times but never wounded, a fact which led many to believe that he wore a shirt of mail.

Tall, extremely agile and gutsy, Bell was now a few years on the down side of thirty. Sandy headed, with flashing blue eyes, he always wore a mustache and a small goatee. His features had once been handsome, but during some wild melee a blow had crushed the cartilage of his nostrils. Now his features were marred by a grotesque button-shaped nose. This rankled him greatly and was ever a sore spot with him. Wisely his associates learned to refrain from staring at his nose or referring to it in any way. Ironically, his bizarre organ of smell would one day bring about his capture and demise.

Due to his medical training Tom Bell soon had many followers who were ready to ride at his stirrup. Where else could an outlaw find a leader who could perform an operation or bind up wounds after a shootout? And, rough though he was in manner and conduct, it was said that he was extremely gentle in all of his "doctoring."

Tom Bell had a flair for mystic codes and other secret doings. This often came in handy. It was about the only practical way of identifying members of Bell's gang (at times there were over fifty members who did outlawry for Bell) at the Mountaineer House, one of the taverns where they hung out. There, any new member would order a drink and nonchalantly display a bullet with a string through it as he was being served. This gimmick served to let the bartenders, saloon girls and the proprietor know that he was one of Tom's "boys" and should be given the hospitality of the establishment.

Two other hideouts used by Bell and his gang were the Western Exchange (known to most as the Hog Ranch on the Nevada City road) and the California House, located just two hours by stage out of Marysville, on the Camptonville Pike. At all of the hideouts the gang could depend upon the proprietors, bartenders and girls to keep them posted on the activities of the local law authorities and to supply them with other information helpful to the gang.

The proprietress of the Hog Ranch was a fat, slobbish, red-haired woman who had three daughters. And one of Elizabeth Hood's three daughters soon became Tom Bell's woman. In her warm, tender arms the outlaw spent much of his time when not otherwise occupied with outlawing and robbing stages.

Like Reelfoot Williams, Bell is also credited by some historians as the outlaw who first organized a gang and robbed a stage. Those particular historians base their opinion on his gang's August 12, 1856 robbery of Sam Langton's Marysville-Camptonville stage. Whether or not it was the first such holdup, it was at least pretty well planned and organized, if not successful. On that date the aforementioned stage pulled into the California House and discharged a passenger. This was Smith Sutton, dressed as a miner, but in reality one of Bell's gang who had been on the stage to learn its strength and whether or not it was carrying any treasure. Slyly Sutton passed word that of the stage's eight or nine passengers at least five were harmless. Four were unarmed Chinese men and the fifth was a Negro woman. Sutton also reported that the stage was carrying at least $100,000 and had but one guard aboard.

Shortly after the stage pulled away Tom Bell and his men hit the saddle. Their plan was to rob the coach at nearby Dry Creek. As the robbers reached the intended spot a Mr. Rideout, local gold dust buyer, came riding down a crossroad. Quickly they disarmed him lest he spoil their plans. Leaving one outlaw to guard Rideout and to watch the horses, Tom Bell and his men drew their guns. They stepped out into the road as the stage approached and ordered that the box be thrown down.

Seeing the masked bandits, John Gear, the driver, pulled up his teams to comply, thinking of his passenger's safety. But Bill Dobson, the gutsy guard, was undaunted by the guns facing him. Quickly he pulled the trigger on his shotgun, knocking Tom Bell from his saddle without causing him serious damage. Nerved by Dobson's action the armed passengers on the stage began to fire. The unexpected resistance forced the outlaws to take cover. While they were scrambling for safety Bill Dobson screamed for the driver to put his teams to flight. When Gear was slow to do so Dobson turned his gun upon him and told him to get moving or get shot! It was only then that Dobson realized the driver was wounded.

As the teams hit the traces and pulled the bouncing stage across the rough terrain, Dobson took stock. The four Chinese had jumped from the coach and taken flight at the first gunshot. But in the hail of lead the Negro woman had taken a stray bullet through the brain and was dead.

The countryside was up in arms when news spread of the daring robbery. Scores of lawmen and armed citizens beat the bushes searching for the bandits, determined to make an example so that it wouldn't happen again. Within three days one man was run to ground and killed, and two other outlaws captured. Tom Bell got the message. The handwriting was on the wall. The country was too hot for him. Overnight people who had formerly given him aid and support turned their backs. He made tracks and left the country.

But his attachment for the Hood girl drew him back. He persuaded the mother and her three daughters to move to his new place on the Merced River. There, Bell and the women settled down and began to make plans for the future.

Meanwhile, some of the lawmen noticed that Bell and the Hood women had disappeared at the same time. Knowing of Bell's affair with the Hood daughter, the lawmen put two and two together and began to look for the women. It was not too hard to track down a big fat, red-headed woman with three daughters in women-rare country. Hiding the four females would have been about as easy as hiding an elephant under a peanut. Soon the lawmen were questioning and threatening Mother Hood and her daughters. And, as such has happened since time began, the women pointed the finger.

On October 6, Tom Bell was astride his horse, talking to a Mexican he had met upon the trail. Suddenly a band of men rounded a bend and approached. Thinking that they were probably deer hunters, Bell paid no mind until the gut-jarring click of hammers being eared back got his attention. He turned to stare into nine gun barrels at close range. There wasn't a chance in the world for him to escape. As they disarmed him and called his name, he began to protest, saying he wasn't Tom Bell. But the leader of the posse, the sheriff of Calaveras County, called attention to the outlaw's nose, an unmistakeable sign of identification. As the posse began to lead him to the nearest tree, Bell admitted his identity. He asked for a chance to write some final letters to his loved ones back in Tennessee and the posse decided to grant his wish.

Four hours later, his letters finished, Tom Bell was hung. At last his debt had been paid to society. Their search completed and duty done, the weary posse reined their mounts around and headed back to the county seat. In their saddlebags rode the letters that would soon bring heartbreak to Dr. Thomas Hodge's loved ones along the banks of the Cumberland . .

Richard Perkins, alias George Brett Lytle, alias Dick Fellows, was undoubtedly the unluckiest outlaw in the history of the old West. Born and reared in a time and place where man's four-legged friend was practically a dire necessity (and often the difference between life and death) it was ironical that he suffered far more from the horses he was involved with than from all the lawmen who aspired to nail his hide to the wall! Because of a horse he broke his leg at a highly inopportune moment; because of a horse he possibly lost out on a $240,000 haul; because of a horse he was eventually captured and sent to prison for life; yet, despite deep humiliation at the hands of (or should we say hooves of?) his four-legged enemies, he kept coming back for more. Truly, horses were his downfall!

Stocky, well-built, and possessed of a rich, curly black beard, Dick Fellows had a lot of guts and pride. And there hardly can be any doubt that he was striving hard to live up to an image, the image of a dashing highwayman racing across the prairies and mountains looting stages, loving fair damsels and thwarting the law at every turn. Such were his fantasies but, unfortunately for him, they never reached fruition. And all probably because horses sensed he was afraid of them and thereby took the upper hand. Today, science has definitely established that any human afraid of a horse, dog, or other animal emits a tell-tale scent that is instantly recognized by the animal concerned. As a result, the animal knows it has the upper hand and reacts accordingly. In all probability such was the case with Dick Fellows. According to the annals of the old West the unfortunate rogue came in second in each encounter he had with his four-legged enemies!

The first news of Dick Fellows as a highwayman resulted when he robbed a horseman near Los Angeles in 1869, then tried to hold up the Coast Line Stage near Santa Barbara. Unsuccessful in the stage robbery, he was immediately run to ground, tried, and sent up to San Quentin on January 31, 1870.

Fellows began to study the Bible and was allowed to organize a Sunday-school class. Soon he was known for his lengthy sermons to fellow prisoners. He was so fervent in his efforts that gradually he was regarded as the leader of the religious element of the institution. Plainly he had seen the error of his ways and was working hard to save his fellow-prisoners from the clutches of Satan!

He was so convincing that several of the prison officials suggested that his sentence be lightened. Others took up his cause as time went by and on April 4th, 1874, Governor Newton Booth granted him an unconditional pardon! It is interesting that on the day of his release the pardoned man shook hands gratefully with all concerned, then conducted a prayer service for those poor unfortunate convicts who dared to hint that he was not sincere in his religious beliefs.

In 1875 Jim Hume was in Caliente, California for the purpose of safeguarding some $240,000 in gold coin to be shipped to Los Angeles. While three large express boxes containing the coin were being loaded on the southbound stage, the ever wary Hume spotted San Quentin's recent graduate among the crowd. Fellows was accompanied by a rough-looking man and the two moved as near the express boxes as they could, obviously curious about the shipment.

At last the shipment and passengers were aboard and ready for the twenty-three hour journey south. Hume climbed to his seat next to the driver and positioned his weapons so they would be convenient if needed. His arsenal consisted of two double-barreled shotguns, two Winchester rifles, and a pair of pistols. Jim Hume was ready!

Dick Fellows and his companion watched the departure of the stage, evaluating their chances of a successful stick-up. Retiring to a nearby red-eye parlor, they discussed the matter and finally decided to go full speed ahead. There was only one problem. Dick Fellows didn't have a horse. It was finally resolved that Dick's companion would ride ahead while Fellows went to the local livery stable and rented a steed. Then Fellows would join his cohort as soon as he could and they would "pull the job."

Finishing their whiskey, the two moved to carry out their plans. But as Fellows was riding his rented horse across the flats it sensed his inability to take charge. The steed went into action. A few minutes later Fellows was limping back to the stable, suffering great pain as the result of landing on his head. Desperately he pondered his situation. By the time he could get the horse back it would be too late to meet his partner at the designated spot and pull the holdup.

The northbound stage from Los Angeles was due to arrive shortly. If he only had a horse he could rob that stage all by himself. And then no one could say that Dick Fellows was a coward! He was entering the main part of town when he saw a horse standing hitched to a rack nearby. He peered around for a moment, making sure no one was watching him. Unlooping the reins from the rack, he put his foot in the stirrup and swung into the saddle. Reining the animal around, he kicked at its ribs and raced out of town. Hey! Everything was going fine. Just proved that all you had to do was to show the four-legged critter who was boss!

It was well nigh to dark as the Los Angeles stage drew near Dick Fellows' hiding place. Gun drawn and cocked he rode into the middle of the dusty trail and ordered the driver to throw down the box. It went well. Two minutes later the Wells Fargo box was on the ground and the stage was disappearing, racing into Caliente, a mile or so away.

Anxiously Fellows dismounted and looked at the box. Suddenly he realized he had no axe or other weapon for opening the chest. His brow wrinkled as he worked at the problem. He had to do something. A posse would be showing up shortly and he had no desire to be found in the vicinity. Ah, there was a way! Slowly he managed to hoist the box and rest it on the saddle horn. Then he put his left foot in the stirrup and started to climb up behind the box. Eyes cocked, trying to figure out what this strange man was doing, the horse stood snorting for a moment. Then it catapulted into the air. Dick Fellows was half-way in the saddle when the mount erupted. Spinning like a top it threw the outlaw and the strongbox into the dust of the trail. Angrily the outlaw lay on his back, his senses reeling as he listened to the sound of hooves fading in the distance toward Caliente.

What to do now? Suddenly he recalled seeing some tunnels and grading that the Southern Pacific Railroad had been doing in the area. If he could carry the heavy strongbox that far and manage to hide out. Slowly he plodded through the total darkness, the heavy green box on his shoulder. Suddenly he was falling through space! For a few moments he thought he would be falling forever. And then he was crumpling as he hit the bottom of the pit, a sharp pain stabbing at his left leg. Waves of hurt swept over him as he fought back nausea and took stock. It was bad. He had broken his left leg just above the ankle and then the box had crushed the instep of the same foot.

For a while he lay there, trying to decide his next move. Many men would have quit, but not Dick Fellows. The memory of San Quentin was still too fresh. He began to crawl, dragging the strongbox behind him. Hours later he passed near a railroad worker's tent. Cautiously he searched until he found an axe. He crawled away so that he wouldn't be heard and used the axe to open the treasure. Inside, he found $1,800 in money. Not the biggest haul from a Wells Fargo box but better than nothing! He stashed the loot in his pockets and crawled on. Finding a small willow sapling, he used the axe to fashion a rough crutch. He threw the axe away and hobbled slowly through the night. In his brain was one roiling thought. He was moving too slow and the crutch would be so easy to track. There was one thing clear . . . He had to get a horse!

James Hume and his shipment had no trouble on their ride to Los Angeles. Anxiously the chief of Wells Fargo detectives was looking forward to a hot bath, a thick steak and a good night's sleep. But it was not to be. When he arrived at the stage stop the local Wells Fargo agent notified him that the northbound stage to Caliente had been robbed just twelve hours after Hume had passed it. Immediately Hume caught the next stagecoach north, his mission—to catch the party or parties involved. And he had a fairly good idea who the guilty parties were!

The following day Hume and an officer named Meyers rented mounts from a Caliente stable and rode to the scene of the holdup. Carefully they searched the area for clues. Hume watched as a youth came riding by, eyes glued on the ground as though looking for something he had lost. It occurred to the detective that the boy might be trying to find the tracks of the stage robber, so he began to question him. He learned that the youth was named Tommy Fountain and that he was searching for a horse stolen from his father's farm the night before. In the course of their conversation Tommy remarked that of three horses the thief could have stolen he had taken the one most easy to track. He explained. A few days before the horse had lost a shoe and his father had nailed a mule shoe on the foot until he could take the horse to a blacksmith.

Hume smiled as he pictured such a print. Could it be that the horse had been stolen by the holdup artist? Or, could it be that the horse had not been stolen at all, but had simply strayed from its pasture? James Hume was not a man to overlook any possibilities. Before he parted from the youth, Tommy Fountain had promised to notify Hume if he found the horse's trail.

Later that day the boy did run across the tracks. As soon as he could he sent word to the detective. Then Tommy headed for nearby Bakersfield to notify the local sheriff.

Hume headed for Bakersfield at once when he received the boy's message, arriving there to see Tommy, the local sheriff, and a dirty, bearded creature on a willow crutch. The bearded man was in much pain and his left leg was swollen so badly that blood poisoning could not be ruled out.

Dick Fellows was hospitalized until his leg healed, then was tried for his crimes. He made a long, impassioned plea for mercy which fell upon deaf ears. Evidently the court was aware of his speech before the parole board. He was sentenced to 8 years in San Quentin.

But something happened . . .

Fellows was being held in a plank building that the city of Bakersfield was using as a temporary jail while a new one was being built. To ensure his safe-keeping, a guard stood watch every night just outside his door. Imagine the jailer's surprise one morning when he opened the door to feed his prisoner and found the cell empty! The slippery outlaw had managed to cut a hole in his cell's wall and slip through. But he had added insult to injury when he used the pair of new crutches the state had given him to hobble away!

Four days later he was recaptured . . . Once again a horse had failed him, leaving him vulnerable and unable to travel further. The determined outlaw had hobbled through the night on his new crutches until he found a barn with a corral full of horses. Cutting one out of the bunch, he had led it some distance away from the corral and tied it to a post. Then he had gone back to the tackshed and groped in the darkness until he found a saddle. But when he hobbled back to the tied horse, intending to cinch the hull down and ride away, he was sadly disappointed. The poor beast was so frightened by the sight of the strange four-legged creature stealing through the night that it reared and broke its halter. Dejectedly Dick Fellows was forced to watch as the horse lashed out with both hind legs, kicking at the air, then galloped back to the barn. Crestfallen, the road agent hobbled back to the barn and bedded down in some loose hay to sleep.

The farmer harnessed his team shortly after daybreak the next morning and drove away. From Fellow's hiding place he heard the man bid his wife goodbye, telling her that he would return from Bakersfield as soon as his business would permit. Hungry, the outlaw straightened his mussy clothes as well as he could, put on his best smile, and rapped on the farmhouse door. When the lady of the house appeared, the crippled man confessed that he had been on his way to Bakersfield but had gotten lost. He wondered if she would be so kind as to give him direction?

Later that day her husband returned, eager to tell her of the sensational outlaw who had broken out of his cell and made his getaway on crutches. Aghast, she interrupted him excitedly; then she launched into an account of the visitor who had called at their house that day.

Once again the family wagon headed for Bakersfield, this time at a much faster clip. The sheriff was informed and two posses were quickly searching the area around the couple's farm. The tell-tale marks of his crutches were soon found and he was recaptured and back in jail before nightfall. Two guards were assigned to keep their eyes on the prisoner that night and the new sheriff arranged to transport his slippery prisoner to prison the very next day. On June 16, 1876, the somber gates of San Quentin clanged shut behind Dick Fellows for the second time.

This time the Bible-class routine didn't work . . .

Resigned to the inevitable, Dick Fellows settled down to serve his sentence. Once again he worked in the prison library; in his spare time he wrote a lot of letters. Jim Hume was the recipient of one of his letters and was somewhat puzzled by its contents. In it, Fellows rambled on, first apologizing to Hume for the trouble he had caused him, then saying that he had never hurt any "small" people in any way; that his entire mission had been to rob from the affluent companies who could well afford the loss. Hume was somewhat confused. It was hard for him to understand why the prisoner expected sympathy and understanding from him since he (Fellows) had repeatedly tried to rob the coffers of Hume's employers.

In May of 1881 Fellows was released from prison. Declaring that he would make a new start, he moved to

Santa Cruz. There he got a job as a solicitor for the *Daily Echo* and tried to teach Spanish on the side. Neither job panned out. On July 10th he robbed the San Luis Obispo-Soledad stage of its strongbox. He was unhappy to find that all it contained was $10. Not much of a haul, but at least he was in business again!

From that time on stages were held up quite regularly in the Santa Clara Valley. Jim Hume studied the reports coming across his desk. The robberies and the M.O.'s involved reminded him of his old acquaintance, Dick Fellows. He sent Captain Aull, into the area, instructing him of Dick Fellows' past record and what the outlaw might be expected to do.

Overnight Dick Fellows, alias G. Brett Lytle, was gone. A week after his flight he was taken prisoner in a ranch barn and held for transportation to San Francisco.

Dick Fellow's was escorted to San José to be delivered into the custody of Captain Aull. As the prisoner and his guard got off the train, Fellows told Constable Burke how much he had appreciated knowing him and that he was truly sorry that they wouldn't be seeing each other anymore. Suddenly Fellows saw a nearby saloon. Shaking his head ruefully, he lamented that the two of them couldn't go in and have a farewell drink. Burke was deeply touched. Suddenly he veered, led his prisoner into the tavern and ordered a bottle be set out. Half an hour later the two were feeling no pain.

At last the bottle was empty. Constable Burke and his prisoner bade their new friends goodbye and departed via the swinging doors. Suddenly Dick Fellows found the opportunity he had been seeking for so long. Viciously he raised both hands high and poleaxed the constable across the back of the neck. Burke went down like a ton of bricks, stunned and barely conscious. How could his good old buddy do this to him? He drew his pistol and squeezed off one shot; and then his former companion was out of sight, blending into the shadows. Sadly Constable Burke got to his feet and staggered toward the distant police station where Captain Aull was awaiting to take custody of the "prisoner"!

There was nothing else to do . . . Captain Aull had to start all over again!

Stealing through the blackness of night, Fellows finally found a hiding place in the barn of a physician. His host, a Dr. Gunckel, discovered the stranger early next morning, and naturally he was somewhat curious. Fellows told the kindly man that he had been somewhat tipsy the night before and had taken shelter in the barn to elude some "rowdies" who had stoned him. Concerned, the good doctor fed him and gave Fellows a well-intended lecture on the evils of John Barleycorn as he was leaving. Hurriedly the outlaw moved on, hoping to evade discovery.

A few hours later Fellows was recaptured and taken to the San José jail. The San José law officers took no chances. Three shifts of guards watched the prisoner every second until he was moved to Santa Barbara to stand trial. The trial didn't take long. The judge sentenced him to spend the rest of his natural life in prison.

That *should* be the end of his story . . .

On April 2nd, 1882, Dick Fellows knocked his jailer down and took his pistol. Quickly the road agent ran from the jail, seeking a means of escape. Outside, he saw a horse grazing nearby, anchored by a long rope. Quickly the getaway artist pulled the picket pin, wrapped a halfhitch around the startled beast's nose, and swung upon its bony back. Shots rang out behind him as he drummed his heels against the thin-slated ribs and headed for freedom!

Poor Dick Fellows! How could he have known the horse had almost died the week before as a result of eating loco weed? Though it had partially recovered, the animal was still too spooky to ride. Suddenly the addle-brained creature went into a fit. For the next few seconds beast and man staged an impromptu wild west show in the streets of Santa Barbara. Frantically Dick Fellows wrapped his arms around the sunfishin' creature's neck, trying to save his own! Suddenly it was all over. The crazy critter lunged high and twisted. Fellows sailed through the air and landed on his back, driving the breath from his tortured body. He offered no resistance at all as he was led back to his jail cell. And so ended the career of Dick Fellows, stage-coach road agent, Bible-class teacher, and jail-break specialist—doomed by a horse to spend the rest of his life behind cold gray iron bars!

Black Bart . . . "Rattlesnake Dick" . . . Tom Bell . . . Dick Fellows . . . Each of them became well-known in their time . . . But there were others who plagued the mighty Wells Fargo Company and other express firms . . .

Dr. Thomas Hodges-Bell was not the only medical man to become entangled in stage robbery. On May 23, 1868, three outlaws robbed the coach traveling from Helena to Salt Lake City. A posse followed the road agents for four hundred miles, finally losing the trail near Boise, Idaho. Then Wells Fargo's detectives entered the picture. Eventually they captured the three bandits and also bagged eleven others who had been working secretively with them. Among these conspirators were a prominent physician and two other men who had held positions as Deputy United States Marshals!

In another case, Dave Opdyke, the very first sheriff of Ada County was discovered to be a road agent who had preyed upon Overland stages. He was tracked down, summarily tried and hanged by a band variously known as the "Avengers" or the "Northwest Night Riders." The object of this band with the colorful names was to curb the repeated depredations of highwaymen, and a number of the stage and express companies reportedly gave it financial support.

Ladies of the evening had their roles to play in the dramas of the four-wheeled stage; in 1858 Dutch Kate, a plumpish, heavily rouged siren from Marysville, indulged in an extended gambling spree. When it was over and she had sobered up she found she had dropped over $2,000 to the tables. In an effort to recoup, she donned riding clothes, gun belt and a mask. Stepping out from brush at the side of a lonely stage trail, she brandished her pistol and ordered the stage to stop and "throw down the box." Quickly the driver complied with both requests, then Dutch Kate waved him to drive on. Breathlessly the fair damsel tore open the box. She was extremely angry when she found it contained just a very few dollars. Such a small return for so much effort! But she was even more angry the following day when she read the newspaper account of her deed and learned she had missed $15,000 that one of the passengers had been hiding in a valise!

It is interesting to note that many stage robbers were captured and dealt with after their first and only holdup. Such was the fate of C.B. Hawley of Globe, Arizona. Having failed in his profession as a stovewood and charcoal dealer, he decided to try his hand at stage robbing. With a partner, Lafayette Grimes he built a stone breastwork to hide behind as they stopped a mule train bearing a bonanza of $5,000. The breastwork was to give them shelter if gunfire should break out.

But the two would-be bandits failed to take into consideration the excessive bravery of the teamster, likeable Andy Hall. When the gunfire broke out it was as a running shootout; when it was over Andy Hall and a Dr. Vail were dead. With his dying words Dr. Vail put names to the men who had done him in, and posses were out posthaste, hunting for Hawley and Grimes. Almost instantly they were caught; and four days after the robbery they were brought before a citizen's committee at Globe's own Stalla's Hall. The prisoners confessed and asked for three hours time to go get the loot and return it. They were granted their request, and with thirty of the committee trekked into the hills and recovered the $5,000.

At 1:45 A.M. the church bells of the little mining town began to chime. All saloons and gambling houses were closed as the citizen's committee escorted the two holdup men to a tall sycamore on Main Street. Solemnly the rites were carried out and Hawley and Grimes paid for their offense.

Fifteen minutes after the necktie party was over the saloons were reopened, the dice rolled and the liquor flowed; and the local barflies had a juicy subject of conversation to last them through the coming winter!

Throughout the gold country the railroads were coming into their own, just as had happened many years before along the eastern seaboard, now the huge black engines with their long strings of cars were replacing the Concord and its six-up. Mining, banking, expressing, even highway robbery was undergoing a change!

Train robberies had become a common occurence back in the Midwest due to the Reno Brothers, Jessie and Frank James, and other early gangs. But it was something that had not been done in Nevada until the morning of November 6, 1870 at approximately 1:45 A.M.

The eastbound Central Pacific train was boarded by a party of men as it made its regular stop at Truckee. The train continued its run until it was stopped abruptly at Verdi, seven miles to the east. Conductor Mitchell was slightly put out at the unscheduled stop; wearily he shook his head, thinking it was probably caused by some carousing miners or some silly brakeman playing a trick.

Swiftly he learned it was no trick. Two bandits climbed into the cab of the train and their hammered-back guns got the engineer's attention. "Keep quiet and obey orders," was their command. Hearing the outlaw's words, the fireman dropped off the other side of the cab and headed for the nearby timber. At the same time several other outlaws climbed into the Express and baggage car and disarmed Marshall, the Wells Fargo messenger. Within a few minutes the bandits had found almost $42,000 and were ready to leave the train. (Ironically they missed several bars of gold bullion which Marshall sneaked into a small pile of firewood near his heating stove.)

The bandits were leery of attempting an escape from the train, aware that there were armed men in the passenger car who might give chase. Suddenly one of the nightriders reached down and pulled the link pin that connected the baggage and passenger cars. Under the threat of guns Engineer Small started his engine and rolled through the night until ordered to stop. Quickly the outlaws disappeared, leaving the engineer, his cab and the baggage car five miles from the rest of the train. Hurriedly engineer Small returned, rehitched his train and proceeded for Reno and help.

Across the gold country a shrill cry of alarm rose from all sides. The *San Francisco Chronicle* summed up their feelings:

> We Americans get terribly indignant when we read of the doings of brigands in Spain, or Greece, or Italy. We wonder how such things can take place in a civilized country. We make no scruples of accusing the government of supineness, or the population of complicity, in the acts of the robbers. We have our own brigandage and it promises to eclipse the European institution in audacity and magnitude. The evil has been developing for a long time and it now has reached a stage where it threatens the welfare of the entire Pacific Coast. From horse-stealing it ascended to stagecoach-plundering and from that it has advanced to seizing and robbing railroad trains. If it continues to progress, the next step will be the sacking and burning of towns.
>
> We trust that energetic steps which are being taken to secure the arrest of the brigands will succeed . . . so that the criminals will either stretch hemp or receive their quietus from the bullets of their pursuer's rifles. If they should escape it will become the duty of the railroad company to send an armed guard with each train, in order to protect the lives and property of the passengers.
>
> Unless this is done there can be no guarantee that the Verdi affair will not be repeated as often as the Knights of the Road think it is necessary to replenish their purses at the expense of the public.

The gauntlet had been thrown, the press had made its charge; now, the countryside was wondering what would be done about the matter?

Early the next day Nels Hammond, Wells Fargo agent at Reno, and Deputy Sheriff Lamb of Washoe were riding through the snow of Sardine Valley, tracking the bandits. Stopping at a small tavern operated by Nicholas Pearson and his wife, Hammond asked if any strangers had been in the area. They were told of two men who had spent the night at the tavern and proceeded that morning for Sierra Valley. Anxiously Hammond and Lamb plunged on. But the Pearsons had neglected to tell the officers of another man who had spent the night at their inn. After the lawmen rode from view this man, Gilchrist, walked out to an outhouse where he stayed for some time. Having learned of the train holdup from Hammond and Lamb, Mrs. Pearson became suspicious of Gilchrist's actions. No shrinking violet, she slipped silently to the side of the outhouse and peeked in through the small knothole. She watched Gilchrist putting bright gold coins into an old boot. Finally he hid the boot in the outhouse and prepared to leave the privy. Quickly Mrs. Pearson slipped back and told her husband who then slipped away to find the local authorities. Finally, after walking about twelve miles, he found Sheriff Kinkead of Reno.

Returning to the Pearson tavern, Kinkead and Pearson found Gilchrist hiding in a barn and made him prisoner. They had not been questioning him for very long before he broke completely. He yielded almost $12,000 in gold coin and named his accomplices. The ringleader had been A. J. "Big Jack" Davis, former superintendent of the San Francisco Mine at Virginia City. A telegram brought about the capture of Davis. He had $19,760 which was his share of the holdup money.

Justice raced through the country. Tilton Cockerill, a former army officer, was arrested along with Sol Jones. Together they had $7,345. Slowly the loot was being recovered.

It was learned that the gang had used coded telegrams to help expedite their robbery. J.E. Chapman, one of the ringleaders had sent a wire from San Francisco saying, "AM SENDING YOU SIXTY DOLLARS." To the gang members the message actually meant that Chapman had learned that the train's express car was carrying $60,000 that was being shipped to the Yellow Jacket Mine to be used as payroll money.

Detectives began searching in the Bay Area for Chapman but could find no trace of the outlaw. Knowing there was a possibility that the fugitive might be in Reno, they caught the next train for that city. (Little did they know at the time that the man they were seeking was riding on the same train, headed for the same place!)

When they arrived at their destination the detectives entered a tavern near the depot to get a sandwich and cold drinks. Suddenly two Reno detectives that they knew walked in; with them was Sol Jones, the bandit who had been captured with Cockerill. The four lawmen were discussing the case when all at once Sol Jones brightened as he stared across the saloon. He waved his hand and called out, "Hey, Chapman! What brings you here?"

His greeting brought J.E. Chapman a prison sentence of 18 years!

The final tally of the Verdi train robbery was as follows; Gilchrist and another man, Roberts, turned state's evidence and went free. Jones, Squires, Cockerill and Parsons drew sentences of 21 years each; but "Big Jack" Davis, their ringleader drew only 10 years. And later a soft-hearted Nevada governor cut that sentence to only 3 years.

As usual, Wells Fargo and the local authorities worked hand-in-hand in solving the case. The gang had been brought to justice, almost all of the gold recovered, and the trains continued to roll through the gold country!

There were many who dared to challenge Wells Fargo's express and banking business by means of stage holdups, train robberies and other nefarious activities.

Some of those who were captured and sent up saw the light and "went straight" after being uncaged from their dreary prison cells; but some others never seemed to learn. Such were the cases of Dick Fellows and "Big Jack" Davis. Fellows was brought to law by horses and "Big Jack" (according to the writer, Neill Wilson) by an error in judgement. Said Wilson in *Treasure Express:*

> He ("Big Jack") died by an error of judgement in '77. His error of judgement was in trying to stop a stage defended by Wells Fargo messengers, Eugene Blair, who never lost a battle, and Jimmy Brown.

CHAPTER
VI

THE DRIVERS
AND
MESSENGERS

"Now, Cal, ye better look right sharp! Ol' John Majors got hisself held up on this run the other mornin' by Jack William's ghost!"

Cal Olmstead grinned at the old man carrying the lantern. As they walked from the Telegraph Stage Company's office, he patted the old-timer on the shoulder and chuckled, "Oh, I will, cause I'm plumb scared o' them spooks of any kind." He walked to the waiting Concord and climbed the three step plates up to the driver's seat. Carefully he gathered up the ribbons, then nodded at the station agent, saying, "Thanks for the coffee. See you on the next run."

He leaned down and called to the six men inside the coach, "Hey, everybody ready?"

"Yeah! Let's go!"

"All right, hang on!" Cal Olmstead yelled like a banshee as he slapped the ribbons against the rumps of his teams. Startled, the six horses dug in, then lunged forward, tightening the traces. The big red coach rocked on its leathers and swung out onto the road, yellow wheels spinning, throwing gravel in its wake. Skillfully, the driver steered through North San Juan's narrow streets, then the stage was out of the little town and heading south, rolling through the shimmering moonlight like some ghostly galleon on wheels!

Suddenly the lead team shied in terror as three masked figures stepped from the chaparral at the edge of the trail. For a moment Cal Olmstead fought his teams, then at last he got them under control. As the pale moonlight bathed the road, it shone on the guns in the intruder's hands.

The driver sized up the situation at a glance. He had no shotgun guard, his hands were full of ribbons, there were six passengers inside the coach whose lives would be jeopardized if the bandits started shooting, and last but not least, one of the masked men had his pistol aimed at the driver—and at this range, he couldn't miss!

Cal Olmstead pulled up his teams.

The leader of the bandits nodded his head, approvingly. "That was smart, Cal!"

The driver stared down at the man. The outlaw had called him by name! Evidently the outlaw knew him!

The outlaw continued, "Now, you just sit there, and don't let your teams spook . . . and you passengers, hey, in there! Get out here and grab air! Now!"

Quickly the other two bandits moved forward, guns ready as the men inside the Concord began to climb out. One of the masked figures searched each passenger for weapons. Finding a pistol in one man's pocket, the bandit shucked the loads from the cylinder and handed it back.

The leader waved his gun authoritatively and spoke again, "Gentlemen, we don't want anything from you. We're here after Wells Fargo's strongbox and we mean to have it!"

There was deep silence as the passengers digested his words. It was obvious that not one of them had any desire to "hero" and risk a bullet in their pelt by trying to save some stranger's gold dust. The leader nodded his head, "That's real smart." He turned to his two men and gestured, "All right, boys. Go ahead and open the box."

One of the outlaws trotted to the side of the trail where

they had first appeared. He groped about in the under-brush, then produced a crow bar and a sledge. Vigorously the two attacked the iron box, while their leader kept the driver and the passengers covered by his pistol. Ten, then fifteen minutes passed; the padlock would not yield. Finally the two outlaws paused. One of them turned to the leader and shrugged his shoulders.

"All right, get it. If we have to use it, we have to." The leader signaled at the brush again.

Once again the man disappeared into the chaparral. When he returned he was carrying a canister of black powder. Wisely, the outlaws carried the treasure box several yards away, reducing the danger from what was to come. Then one of them set a small charge of powder around the lock. There was a loud "whoosh," but still the padlock would not give. Once again the outlaw brought out the can of powder. This time a large amount was tamped around the unyielding lock. The fuse was lit and slowly the flame from the match burned its way across the ground and reached the black powder. There was a large explosion as the box leaped high in the air and the teams threatened to run away. When the smoke was cleared, the lock was twisted in two.

Triumphantly, the leader walked to its side. For a moment he probed its depths, then pulled out a large buckskin bag. With an effort he raised it high, laughing as he did so.

The strongbox had been emptied, now the outlaws were ready to leave. "Here, gentlemen," the leader was holding a bottle of whiskey, offering it to the passenger nearest him. "Everybody have a little snort, it'll help ease you a little."

Quickly the bottle made its round. The chill of the night air and the shock of the holdup had served to put the passengers on edge. Now they drank long and deep, as they watched the bandits prepare to leave.

"Go ahead, gentlemen, finish it. It's a little present from me to you. We'll be seeing you again. Goodnight."

The driver and passengers watched as the masked man backed slowly to the edge of the trail. He raised his hand in a gesture of salute, then he was lost amid the tangled underbrush.

Nobody moved for a few seconds . . .

Sheriff Gentry was sopping hot breakfast biscuits in cream gravy when he heard the sound of running feet on his front porch. Immediately someone rapped loudly on his door, demanding his attention. The sheriff's brow furrowed. Such haste could only mean bad news, he thought to himself. He grabbed his hat and six-gun as he passed the mantelpiece.

Fifteen minutes later he was standing on the jail porch, selecting his posse from the crowd milling about him. Five men and himself. That's all he needed.

Gruffly he swore in his men and they hurried to get their mounts. Five minutes later the six men crawled up into leather. Ignoring the scattered cries of advice and encouragement of the crowd, the old lawman wheeled his sorrel gelding and led his posse toward the scene of the holdup.

As they rode, the sheriff's memory recounted the various crimes that had been blamed upon the outlaw known as Jack William's ghost. The outlaw was sneaky, whoever he was.

Suddenly the lawman reined in his mount. The stage had been held up about fifty yards ahead and he didn't want his men to ride up and mess the sign. He signaled to his men and they dismounted. Each man tied his horse to a bush or tree and then the group moved nearer the holdup site.

Steven Venard moved up to where the stage had been stopped. For a long time he stood still, reconstructing the events that had occurred. Gradually he moved back and forth, his keen eyes filing footprints, studying the black powder canister that had been left behind, and the place where the outlaws had disappeared into the brush.

He turned to the sheriff. "Sheriff Gentry, it's pretty clear. The three of them left the trail here. Then they split up, two of them going straight ahead, while the other man angled off to the right. But I'd bet that pretty soon they will all three get back together." He waited, his cool, gray eyes studying the lawman.

The sheriff moved forward and studied the sign. He nodded. It all made sense, the way Venard had laid it out. He turned and pointed at the first three deputies. "All right, you three and me. We'll follow the two of them that went this way, and Jim," he addressed the fourth man, "you go with Steve, and y'all can handle the other jasper. But men, watch out in there. That brush can be rough on a man in more ways than one."

Turning, he moved into the clawing undergrowth, followed by the other three. Quickly they were out of sight.

Steve Venard stalked through the maze of head-high chaparral, trying to dodge the stinging branches that fought his forward progress. He carried his rifle in his "off" hand, holding it so that nothing could spike the Henry's barrel. He'd known a fellow who had gotten careless in a place like this; when the man had finally had to shoot, the gunbarrel had blown up in his face!

A good hard rain had fallen two nights before. Now the outlaw's tracks were clearcut and easy to follow. Slowly Steve Venard made his way, trailed closely by the other deputy.

Suddenly Venard halted. He pointed to the sign, whispering, "See, he's started angling over to the right; gonna head downstream. Say," suddenly the tracker had a thought, "Jim, if you will go back and get our horses and ride over to Black's Crossing and hide out, I'll get in behind this dude and drive him out to you." He eyed the other man, awaiting his reaction.

Jim nodded his head as he visualized Venard's plan. He grinned, "Yeah, that make's good sense. All right,

Steve, I'll do it and be waitin' for you." Quickly the deputy turned and began to retrace his path. In a moment he was out of sight.

The footprints were much sharper, now, and over here the fugitive had rested for a while, his head cushioned on a sack of some kind, probably the buckskin sack from the Wells Fargo strongbox. The man, whoever he was, was pretty sure of himself, obviously expecting no pursuit. The deputy shook his head, grimly. His years of service as a town marshal, had taught him that sooner or later almost all outlaws got to the point where they got careless; then, usually, they got dead!

Suddenly there was a flash of color before him! A dozen feet in front of him was the outlaw! Venard started to call to the man to throw down his gun, but there was no chance. The man's startled glance was twisting into a deadly grimace as he lifted a Navy Colt to fire at the deputy. Then two shots rang out. For a brief instant the lawman glanced to his left. There! Up there on top of that little ridge was another man. Then his glance was flicking back to the outlaw in front of him: He noted the big hole in the man's chest, saw the sudden current of red gushing forth!

Quickly the deputy spun around, bringing his sights to bear on the second outlaw. The outlaw fired, and lead splattered from a boulder at Venard's side, then his slug tore into the outlaw's skull, driving the life from his body.

The echoes were still ringing through the little canyon. Two of the outlaws were here; the third must be close! Suddenly a deadly slug ricochetted from the stone pillar at Venard's left and whined into the distance. The deputy dived forward, landing on his belly behind some brush. Where was he? Up there, see the little movement of the bushes behind that big rock? Venard studied the situation a moment. This could be like hunting a squirrel. But the first thing is, you got to get his attention! Slyly the deputy cocked his Henry. Picking up a small rock, he tossed it into the bushes behind the third outlaw's hiding place. Startled

the man spun around, triggering a shot. Then he realized he'd been out-foxed. As he whirled to face the deputy he pulled the trigger, but his bullet arched harmlessly into the blue as Steve Venard's shot went true!

The posse found Venard resting on the money bags. A few yards away were the bodies of Jack William's ghost, the alias of George Shanks, a waiter from the Camptonville Hotel, Robert Finn alias Kerrigan, and George Moore, a recent escapee from the state pen. Each of the men had had at least one clear shot at Venard and had missed. The sheriff reviewed the facts; the stage had been robbed about 4:30 that morning, it was now noon, and all of Wells Fargo's money would be returned by 2 P.M.!

In appreciation of Venard's heroism, Wells Fargo awarded him $3,000 and, a handsome Henry rifle, engraved with a drawing of the exploit and the inscription ". . . for his gallant conduct May 16, 1866 . . ."

In the early days of the West very few stages had guards, later referred to as messengers. Usually the driver was armed, but in most cases he couldn't be expected to have a running gunfight while driving four to six head of spooky horseflesh!

The driver was many things; his was a skill that couldn't be learned overnight; the fine art of manipulating six ribbons (or checklines) at the same time, thereby steering six horses along narrow mountain trails or other dangerous terrain.

When his stage was navigating an area where no stage stations existed (whether due to being burned out or not yet built), he was the cook at mealtime; when one of his passengers or horses was sick or wounded, his was the role of doctor or veterinarian (with probably the same rough treatment for either patient).

From the very first days of stagecoaching, the driver was accorded an awe and respect enjoyed by few others. It was he who determined who should have the privilege of riding atop the coach next to him. And Heaven help the poor misguided wretch who crawled into that seat without an invitation!

Stage drivers in general, Hi Washburn in particular, were often content to accept silently criticism as well as adulation from their passengers. However, from time to time they found it necessary to give a little object lesson to demonstrate their qualifications.

The story has been told often, how Washburn found himself confronted with an unwanted, talkative young eastern dandy. Washburn bore up silently under the dude's criticism of the Rocky Mountain scenery, the roads, the horses, the coach, but finally the fatal error was made!

The capper came when the young trespasser asked the driver to "touch up" the horses a bit, saying that "back home in good old Pennsylvania the stages always made marvelous time." The veteran ribbon handler ruminated on those words as the big Concord was drawn to the top of the next steep mountain. There he stopped the coach and asked everyone but the dude to get inside. Having heard the conversation and suspecting the driver's motives, the passengers were quite happy to oblige.

Suddenly the driver screamed like an apache as he lashed his teams down the four-mile grade. Back and forth the stage rocketed on the narrow mountain road, often taking curves on two wheels. The dude whitened. He begged Hi to please, please slow down. But the grizzled driver continued to whip his teams, saying, "Why, this is the way we always come down off this here hill!"

When the stage pulled into the stage station the trembling dude got off, still frightened and hardly able to stand. He stayed a few days as he had intended, but when it was time to make the return trip, he arranged to make the trip by pack mule!

When the "Iron Horse" began to replace the Concords and six-ups along the eastern seaboard, many veteran drivers were put out of work. Luckily for some, there was need for their services in Mexico. Mexican drivers could not get the "hang" of driving a six-up. As a result they used three drivers for each, one man riding one of the horses in each team and steering as he would a saddle horse. Obviously, this method was more costly, tired out the horses and slowed their progress.

When Don Jose Sartuso set up a mail route, he didn't like that method of driving. He got in touch with Abbott and Downing, requesting coaches, harness, and their help in getting him the best American drivers available. At that time the going rate for good drivers was $2 per day in New England. The Don, anxious to get good men and solve his problems, offered $100 per month, plus expenses. Soon he had all the drivers he needed.

Driver's wages, like everything else, went up when gold was found in California. Henry C. Ward, one of the early drivers for Whistman's stage lines, described the situation:

> Drivers salary on the San Jose and San Fran road was $300.00 per month but that was a small part of their income as the perqusetes was big. There was No Mail or Express at the time (1849 and 1850) and the drivers received pay for all letters & packages besides one per cent for all Money carried by them; letters left at the office 25 cts, if delivered $1.00, an erand Nt less than $1.00., passenger way fare $1.00 or less went to the driver. Passengers riding on the seat with the driver was supposed to treat the driver to drinks and cigars on the road. Drinks was free to drivers at all stations but it was seldom that driver drank on the road.

Perhaps the drivers that Ward knew didn't drink, but it is indeed doubtful if the majority of the jehus passed up a little "warmer-upper" on a cold, wintry night!

Schuyler Colfax paid one of the greatest tributes to stage drivers after traveling with editor Samual Bowles' party. Said Colfax: I believe it requires "more talent to drive a stage down the Sierras as we were driven than to be a member of Congress."

Bowles, the distinguished editor of the Springfield, Massachussetts *Republican* added:

> Many a moment we held our fainting breath at what seemed great risks or dare-devil performances ... There is no stage-riding, no stage-driving left in the states—I doubt if there ever was any—at all comparable to this in perfection of discipline, in celerity and comfort, and in manipulation of the reins ... For a week at least we worshipped our knights of the whip. Think, too, of a stageroad one hundred miles long, from Carson to Placerville, watered as city streets are watered, to lay the dust for the traveller!

The experiences of the stagedrivers ranged from laugh-provoking comedy to sheer tragedy ...

One bright morning in 1874, the outbound stage from Hollister was held up by a pair of bandits. The taller and older of the two was an epileptic and the driver was quite concerned that the man's shaky trigger might be his undoing. Carefully, the jehu obeyed the man's every whim. The younger bandit was obviously a girl, with all the right equipment in all the right places. After the pair had stolen the New Idria Mine's payroll, they waved for the unhappy driver to take his stage and leave.

On the driver's return trip that afternoon, the same couple stepped out of the same hiding place along the trail and proceeded to rob him again! It was too much for the driver to take. Like a flash, he sailed his whip through the air, wrapping it around the barrel of the shotgun. He jerked it from the epileptic's hands, disarming him, then wheeled to the young girl. Frightened, she surrendered immediately. The driver used a rope and trussed the outlaws, then delivered them to the local sheriff for safekeeping. And that was the finish of Fred Wilson and Lizzie Keith as stagerobbers!

On occasion, a driver was more concerned with company policy considering the circumstances. Ben Wing was handling a coach out of Salt Lake City carrying two lawmen and a prisoner. The criminal had his sentence permanently reduced when he tried to escape. The deputies, seeing no purpose in delivering a dead prisoner to serve a prison sentence, requested the use of the shovel (carried to free coach wheels that occasionally became caught in the "road"). The driver protested, stating that his bill of lading called for him to deliver the prisoner to his destination. Although the deputies argued, Ben would not depart from his interpretation of the stage line's policy. Company management may have changed their orders after the furor created when the dead man disembarked in downtown Salt Lake City.

A few of the drivers found it necessary to present a certain "image." Like the Californian who was "usually clad in a yellow overcoat, tailor-made yellow trousers with a stripe down the side, a red waist-coat, and high-heeled shoes that made him seem even taller than his natural six feet. Topping off his sartorial splendor was a huge watch and silver chain."

Most were not so fussy about their wardrobe—like hard-working John Craddock. He drove the Marysville-Shasta route for ten danger-laden years, spending so much time on the road that for days at a time he didn't crawl into a bed. Often he would be seen grabbing forty winks in a chair in some hotel lobby while waiting to hit the road again. Craddock left quite a record. He was never late; never had his stage overturned; and was never successfully held up!

One heroic driving achievement was by a passenger who took control of the reins after the driver was the victim of a Indian arrow. The passenger, a 60-year-old judge enroute to Washington, D.C. to serve in the halls of Congress as Nevada's Representative, had to crawl out of the window of the run-away stage and work his way to the drivers box. He successfully avoided further Indian harrassment and drove the stage on to the next station where he humbly relinquished any further driving to the professionals.

114

One driver, named "Baldy" Green, was held up so many times that the phrase "throw down that box, Baldy" became a popular saying of the day, and was eventually made into a song. Green finally retired to the northwest part of the country and became a highly respected Justice of the Peace.

Not all of the drivers were "good guys" . . .

"Frank Williams" loaded his passengers in front of the Virginia Hotel. He seemed to be exceptionally helpful and cheerful as he greeted and loaded their baggage. His manner exuded confidence and reliability as he started the southbound stage on it's way.

As the coach was entering Portneuf Canyon, the scene of several robberies, the passengers heard their driver call out, "Here they are, boys!" Instantly the stage was surrounded by seven masked men, demanding the passenger's money and valuables. Suddenly shooting broke out and the air was filled with lead. When it was over, four passengers were dead, the coach riddled, and $70,000 stolen. The seven bandits had faded into the

distance, the treacherous stagedriver riding at their side! But justice prevailed. The driver was tracked through the Rockies and eventually to Denver, where he was captured. After a brief trial, "Frank Williams," alias Bob Martin, former pony express rider, was hanged one sunny morning along the banks of peaceful little Cherry Creek. He was one of the very few drivers to betray his trust!

Although driving stages and guarding the strongbox was an adventurous undertaking other express company employees found occasional incidents that motivated them to consider those positions safe jobs indeed!

In the spring of 1866 at San Francisco, freight Clerk Haven of Wells Fargo received a leaking box that had recently arrived on the *Sacramento*. He consulted with freight clerk Webster, and the two men decided to open the box to see if it's contents could be salvaged. As they began prying open the lid, presumably using hammer and chisel, the neighborhood was rocked by a gigantic blast. Bodies were blown through the roof, maimed beyond identification, and decapitated, while the building was demolished. The final toll was 10 dead, and 11 seriously injured.

Wells Fargo officials were stunned. What had caused the explosion?

Thirteen days later a ship was being unloaded in Aspinwall, Panama. Again a leaking crate exploded, killing 60 people, burning the steamer, and wrecking every house in the little town.

That was enough for Wells Fargo. Until that time the company had accepted all kinds of freight, be it large, small, hard, soft, or whatever. Immediately the company's officers issued a new set of rules:

> Camphene, nitroglycerine, naptha, benzine, petroleum, or other explosive burning fluids; gunpowder, giant powder, oil of vitriol, nitric or other chemical acids; turpentine, matches, phosphorous, or loaded firearms, Must Not be received for transportation.

The explosion in the Wells Fargo express courtyard was one of the worst tragedies in the company's history. Contrary to some stories the leaky crate was not delivered to Wells Fargo's express offices on a Friday the 13th. It was delivered to the express office on Monday the 16th. However, it could be that the ship bearing the Cargo did dock the previous Friday—the 13th!

Undoubtedly, the most famous of all stagedrivers was Hank Monk. He was the driver who made a wild trip across the rugged Sierras in 1862 with Horace Greeley as his passenger. The famous editor and newspaperman had requested Monk to get him to Placerville in time to present a lecture there. (Mark Twain once said that he had heard this story either 861 or 862 times.) But as the big red Concord careened across the narrow, dangerous trails on two wheels, Greeley began to doubt the wisdom of so much speed. Finally the wealthy businessman began to implore the rough-edged jehu to slow down. But Hank, a colorful individual who believed in saying what he thought, grinned and whipped up his teams a little more, saying, "Keep your seat, Horace, I'll get you there on time!"

When he died, the *Virginia City Enterprise* printed the following story about the veteran driver:

> Hank Monk.—The famous stage driver is dead. He has been on the down grade for some time. On Wednesday his foot lost its final hold on the brake and his coach could not be stopped until, battered and broken on a sharp turn, it went over into the canyon, black and deep, which we call death. In his way, Hank Monk was a character. In the old days, before the leathers under his coach were soaked with alcohol, there was no better balanced head than his. There was an air about him which his closest friends could not understand. There was something which seemed to say that stage driving was not his intended walk; that if he pleased, there were other things, even more difficult than handling six wild horses, which he

could do quite as well. In his prime he would turn a six horse coach in the street with the team at a full run, and with every line apparently loose. But the coach would always bring up in exactly the spot that the most careful driver would have tried to bring it. His eye never deceived him and his estimation of distance was absolute; the result which must be when leaders, swings and wheelers all were playing their roles, with him an exact science. His driving was such a perfection of art that it did not seem art at all, and many an envious whip, watching him, has he turned away to say "He is the luckiest man that ever climbed on top of a box."

It was not luck at all, it was simply an intuitive, exact calculation from cause to effect, and his whole duty ended when he fixed the cause. The effect had to be. He has often driven from the summit of the Sierra down into the valley, ten miles, in forty-five minutes. Other drivers have done as well, the only difference being that with others it was a strain upon the eye and hand and arm and foot; with Monk it was a matter of course. He was to stage driving what the German papers say Edwin Booth was to *Hamlet,* "It was not played, but lived."

As time passed, more and more highwaymen turned to looting stages in an effort to get the precious metals riding in Wells Fargo's treasure chests. In an effort to defend their boxes, the company began to increase the use of shotgun guards (messengers). It was the messenger's duty to ride atop the box at the left of the driver—unless the driver was left-handed, in that case the guard rode on the right side—with the familiar green Wells Fargo box between his feet. His was the obligation to protect the chest at all costs.

One of the brave men who served in that capacity was the illustrious Bret Harte.

Harte came west in 1857 when he was just 21. Soon he went to work for Wells Fargo, riding shotgun on stages in the counties of Humboldt, Trinity, and Siskiyou. Finally

tiring of the job, he turned to school-teaching for a while until the itch to write grew too strong. In his story, "A Night At Wingdam," he pictures a Wells Fargo messenger:

> The gallant expressman, who knew everybody's Christian name along the route, who rained letters, bundles, and newspapers from the top of the stage, whose legs frequently appeared in frightful proximity to the wheels, who got on and off while we were going at full speed, whose gallantry, energy, and superior knowledge of travel crushed all us other passengers to envious silence . . . I stood gloomily, clutching my shawl and carpet bag, and watched the stage roll away, taking a parting look at the gallant expressman as he hung on the top with one leg, and lit his cigar from the pipe of a running footman . . .

In 1880, fearless Mike Tovey, one of the most famous shotgun guards, was serving on the Carson-Bodie line. When a stagecoach was robbed, Tovey rode to the scene of the crime on another coach, then got down on the ground to look for sign. He was walking slowly, tracking the outlaws by the light of a lantern he was carrying, when shots rang out from the blackness of the night. They missed Tovey narrowly, but killed one of the stage horses just behind him. Quickly the messenger returned the outlaw's fire, shooting at their gun-flashes and cursing voices. He killed one desperado and the other one fled into the night.

One day in April of 1892, Tovey was riding shotgun on the San Andreas stage, enroute to the Sheep Ranch in Calaveras County. Riding between Tovey and the driver was a lovely young girl who was enjoying the scenery along the route. Suddenly a deadly hail of buckshot winged through the air, killing the young girl and the driver, and wounding Tovey in one hand. Bravely, Tovey gathered up the ribbons with his other hand and drove the coach and its other passengers to safety.

In January of 1893, Mike Tovey was killed by a road agent in Amador County who undoubtedly knew he was in the box. Knowing Tovey's reputation, the bandit realized his only opportunity for success lay in dispatching the guard immediately.

Phil Barnhart pulled one of the slickest surprises ever on a bandit in 1876. Barnhart was the shotgun guard on a stage running between two early day boomtowns vainly trying to make the adjustment to respectability. Barnhart complied with the bandit's request to throw down the strongbox, but while the talkative outlaw was "shootin' the breeze" with the driver, he slipped off his seat, went behind the stage and potted the road agent. The explosion of his double-barreled shotgun frightened the teams, whose checklines were loose and on the ground, and they ran away, stage, driver, passengers and all. Making sure that the outlaw was dead, Barnhart hoisted the Wells Farbo box to his shoulder and trudged the six miles to the station where he rejoined his stage and continued his assignment!

A similar ruse was pulled on another "baddie" by John McNemer, guard on the Shasta-Weaverville stage in October of 1876. After the box was thrown down as per his command, the bandit ordered the coach to drive on. But when it was out of the masked man's sight and hearing, McNemer jumped off and sneaked back through the maze of underbrush. The nervy guard arrived just as the bandit was prying open the box. Seeing the messenger, the bandit grabbed for his gun. He was a little too slow. He was identified as the robber who had plagued several stages in the northern part of California.

Eugene Blair was one of the bravest and finest of all shotgun guards. On September 4, 1870, Blair and Shotgun Jimmy Brown were the messengers on a stage carrying a valuable payroll to Tybo mining camp. Four ex-cons held up Willow Stage Station (where the payroll-laden stage was scheduled to stop) and tied up its station agent and his crew, and hid out around the station, waiting for the coach.

When the stage arrived that night, its driver, guards and passengers tired and hungry, were looking forward to a cup of coffee and a meal. As Blair started to jump down from his perch, a voice rang out from the darkness, warning all to raise their hands to the sky. Instantly Blair jumped the bandit. The outlaw aimed at the guard's head, but Blair knocked the gun down just in time. Back and forth they wrestled, while Shotgun Jimmy Brown kept his weapon ready, hoping for a shot. Finally the rays of a lantern hanging on the stable wall revealed the outlaw as he and Blair were parted momentarily. Wham! Nine heavy slugs of lethal buckshot tore the life from the outlaw's body, and he fell like a poled ox!

The other outlaws fired, shattering Shotgun Jimmy's leg, then they fled into the haven of the darkness. But they did not enjoy freedom long. They were captured the following day and made to pay for their crime.

The express companies and stage lines could not depend on the guards and messengers entirely, however, and from time-to-time citizens found it necessary to take the matter of law enforcement into their own hands. The episodes where vigilante groups were effective in curtailing crime waves in their areas are numerous. Their tactics are no better demonstrated than this bit of doggrel that was attached to the graves of three "convicted" highwaymen:

> Here lies the body of Allen, Curry and Hall;
> Like other thieves they had their rise, decline and fall,
> On yon pine tree they hung til dead,
> And here they found a lonely bed,
> We're bound to stop this business, or hang you to a man,
> For we've hemp and hands enough in town, to swing the whole damn clan.

It might not have been Shakespeare, but it sure carried a message . . .

In time, the coming of the "Iron Horse" caused many of the stage messengers to leave the stagecoaches for the railroad's express cars. The most famous messenger to serve both was Aaron Y. Ross. He had spent many years as a stage guard in the states of Idaho, Montana, and Nevada. Now he plied his trade as messenger for the Central Pacific.

He was serving as messenger January 21st, 1883, when several robbers held up the train. When he noticed the train slowing down, Ross reasoned that it had reached its destination and started to open the doors of his express car. He saw the bandits in the nick of time and slammed the door closed. The robbers fired at him, ordering him to give up, but he fired back and refused them.

Gunfire rang out for several minutes but the gutsy guard gave as good as he got. Finally the outlaws detached the train's cab and another car from the baggage car and the rest of the train, planning to use the engine and other car as a battering ram to cave in one end of the messenger's car. Although they succeeded in giving him quite a headache, still Ross would not surrender his safe.

The robbers had another idea. This time they took some picks from the railroad's tool supply and started digging a hole in the side of the messenger's car. But his bullets made them change their mind. They quit that venture pronto. One bright outlaw decided they should burn him out. But the express car wouldn't burn. Still another bandit crawled atop the express car and crept along, trying to find a hole so that he could potshot the messenger. Ross sent some bullets through the roof and the man took a flying leap from the top of the car, deciding it was a very poor place for his health!

At last the bandits gave up. But as they disappeared, several of the train's passengers said that it seemed that at least two of them had been wounded by the messenger's bullets.

Ross was the man of the hour. He had suffered two flesh wounds, another bullet had passed through his clothing, but he had stood the robbers off for three hours, and possibly wounded two. He was written up for his deed in every newspaper across the country, and given $1,000 by Wells Fargo. In addition, they presented him with a beautifully engraved gold watch. Many times Ross was challenged by robbers. But never in his entire career did he yield a Wells Fargo strongbox or give up its treasure. His record was truly one of the greatest of all!

Several years later, messenger Charles D. Baxter pulled a nice surprise on a pair of enterprising bandits one night. They had stopped the Chicago-Burlington-Quincy train and ordered Baxter to toss out his safe. When he refused, the robbers forced the engineer to uncouple the express car and move it a short distance away, so they could use dynamite to blast open its door. But Baxter had surmised what the robbers had in mind. While they were busy getting the car moved, he sneaked out its door with his shotgun and hid in a nearby ditch. He waited until the bandits were busy setting their charge, then cut loose. His deadly buckshot killed one outlaw instantly and put the other to flight. And another robbery attempted had been aborted, another express treasure saved.

CHAPTER
VII

32 YEARS
OF
GREATNESS!

Wells Fargo's development had been so rapid that the company was suffering from "growing pains." Its far-flung empire, now almost 20 years old, covered several states, included banks, express offices, stage-coach lines and shipping routes, and was responsible for the safety of human cargoes as well as the depositing, shipping, and safekeeping of gold, and finally, the delivery of mail.

The company had been involved with huge sums of money for so long that its name had become synonymous with riches and great wealth. With such a reputation it was only natural that it was the target of every bandit in the territory, whether the two-bit variety or the real live blood and thunder shoot-'em-up gangs. As a result, the executives of the company had been searching for some time to find a man truly capable of heading up their detective agency.

James B. Hume impressed them greatly. Lloyd Tevis and John J. Valentine, the active heads of the company, had studied his record as a law enforcement officer, and when Hume was defeated in a political election and ousted from office, they offered him the position of Chief of Detectives.

He accepted their offer on one condition; that he first be given a year's leave of absence so that he could accept the job of Deputy Warden of the Nevada State Prison. That institution had suffered a disastrous prison break on September 17, 1871, when thirty prisoners had escaped after attacking the state's lieutenant governor and killing several guards and citizens. Hume's public conscience was such that he could not turn down Nevada's plea to reorganize their prison system and restore order.

Wells Fargo, aware that they had found the right man for the job, agreed to the unusual terms.

When Hume reached Carson City the former warden had been released, leaving a host of problems for the newcomer. Four desperate criminals escaped in September, 1872, and it was Hume personally who left his desk to travel to California and capture two of the men, then to Oregon where he apprehended another, and finally, to Utah where he captured the fourth escapee. He returned each of the prisoners to prison in chains, and upon his return to Carson City instigated a "cleaning up" process that revolutionized the prison.

Following his year's service at the Nevada State Prison, Hume journeyed to Sacramento where he took over as the head of Wells Fargo's detective department as per his contract. There he encountered an unusual problem. Wells Fargo had grown so fast that there was much thievery inside the company by some of its tellers and agents. In order to provide Hume with a "cover" he was usually referred to as Special Officer rather than Chief of Detectives. By this means he was often able to pose as an efficiency expert, making it much easier to conduct certain investigations.

It was soon apparent to Wells Fargo that they had chosen the right man to head their detective department. Hume was familiar with the West, having traveled most of it during his years as a peace officer and miner, his reputation had earned him the respect of the lawmen in the territory and they were always eager to work with him and help in any way. He knew many of the potential lawbreakers and often their M.O.'s or *modi operandi,* and last, but certainly not least, he knew the art of criminal detection and deduction better than any other man in the territory. Add to the above qualities an almost fanatical desire to *always* get his man and you have a fair idea of what made Jim Hume tick!

His first major case came with Wells Fargo started Sunday, July 23, 1873, when four highwaymen held up a Wells Fargo stage between Colfax and Grass Valley and relieved it of $7,788 in gold coin. The bandits herded the twelve passengers and two drivers from the stage and attempted to loot the strongbox which was built into the rear of the coach. Unable to open one lock, the gang prepared to blast it open. Suddenly a female passenger asked if she could have her trunk be removed from the top of the stage to save her belongings from possible damage.

The gallant bandit leader readily complied. He climbed atop the stage and handed the luggage to one of the others who carried it to safety a few yards from the stage. Suddenly a gust of wind blew the leader's mask to one side, briefly revealing his features to the young woman.

A few moments later the powder exploded, blowing part of the strongbox and its lid through the top of the stage. Swiftly the outlaws ransacked the strongbox and disappeared into the brush at the side of the trail.

Surprisingly the coach was still in good condition although its interior had been ruined. Quickly the teams were rehitched, the passengers put back on board and driven to Grass Valley.

At the edge of the little village the driver stopped as per request of his female passenger at the home where she was to board during her stay in Grass Valley. After discharging his passenger, the driver drove on into the town to report the hold-up. Quickly the news was sent to James Hume in Sacramento who hastened to the scene of the crime.

The next day Hume arrived in Grass Valley and began his investigation. During the course of his inquiries he visited the small house where the stage driver had left Eleanor Webber, the female passenger. Hume was surprised to find her gone. The lady of the house filled him in on the previous evening's happenings.

For some time Eleanor Webber had carried on a mail correspondence from back east with a Grass Valley man whom she had never seen. Their letters had resulted in a proposal of marriage from the young man which Miss Webber accepted.

When the young lady arrived, tired and worn out from the long trip and the shock of the holdup, had bathed and rested for a little while. Louis Dreibelbis appeared that evening and preparations were made in order to have the ceremony performed that same evening.

At the ceremony, held by the dim light of a coal-oil lamp, she was introduced to her future husband for the first time. The ceremony was performed. Once the rites were over and the newlyweds embraced, the new bride burst into tears and ran from the room, locking herself in her room, refusing to come out. She left Grass Valley on the first stage next day.

Gravely Hume listened as the puzzled landlady told the story. When she had finished he thanked her for her cooperation and left to continue his investigation.

Later he arrested Charles Thompson, alias Bill Early, for his part in the robbery. Vigorously the suspect denied all charges but under Hume's skillful interrogation he suddenly reversed his story and confessed to the Grass Valley stage robbery and the holdup of the Downieville stage the previous June 23.

Two weeks later Hume got a tip from a friend concerning a young, seemingly prosperous, young man who had begun recently to "drown his sorrows" at the local saloons. It had been discovered accidentally that stories he had told were false.

Hume's curiosity was aroused. Immediately he began checking the man's story himself. The tip proved accurate. The man, calling himself Robert Walker, had never worked for the St. Patrick Mine, and, what's more, his landlady informed Hume that she was holding a gold bar and some coins for the man. The gold bar was identified as having been taken in the Downieville robbery, and the gold coins were blackened as though they had been in a recent explosion.

Hume arrested Walker who confessed, confirming that Charles Thompson had been involved in the robbery and implicating three other men, Nat Stover, a miner, James Meyers, a Grass Valley saloonkeeper, and George Lane, alias George Lester.

Hume and the sheriff of Nevada County arrested Stover and Meyers in Grass Valley and Lane in Virginia City.

Hume's first case for Wells Fargo had been extremely successful. As a result of his diligence and efforts, four of the criminals were apprehended and sent to prison. The fifth (the man masquerading as Robert Walker) turned state's evidence and in return for his cooperation in helping break the case, had been set free.

One strange bit of information emerged from the trials: Robert Walker was in reality Louis Dreibelbis, the missing bridegroom whose wife had rejected him after their wedding ceremony! It was revealed that when she first saw Dreibelbis in the dim lamp light his voice had sounded familiar for some unknown reason. But as they were embracing at the end of their wedding ceremony she recognized him as the outlaw leader who had robbed the stage!

Dreibelbis was released following the trials and returned to Galena, Illinois. Incidentally it was Jim Hume who dug into his own pocket to provide Dreibelbis with transportation and food for his trip back home, and some money to make a brand new start! During the next thirty-two years that Hume served Wells Fargo he helped several former convicts financially; often he even went to government agencies to plead for a lighter sentence for some man whom he felt deserved some special consideration. Hume was relentless when on a case, a man who never gave up, yet his makeup was tempered with mercy for his fellow man, a fact that was to be proven many times!

James B. Hume was born January 23, 1827, in Stamford Township, Delaware County, New York. He grew up on a rough farm, the second youngest of ten children. His father was a strict man who had "no time for nonsense." Shoes, overalls, toys (if any), chores, and even religious

habits were handed down from the eldest to the youngest in the Hume family. Due to their parent's religious zeal and strictness the family rose early, breakfasted by 6 A.M., worked hard all day until dark, then, after a skimpy meal, said their prayers and went to bed early, often still hungry.

When young Jim was 10 his family moved to a part of Indiana known as Pretty Prairie, almost on the Michigan state line and just 25 miles west of Ohio. During the trip west the youth first tasted watermelon, an experience that he remembered throughout his life. Unfortunately the family had chosen a bad time to pull up stakes and move. The depression of '37 fell across the land, drying up

money supplies and reducing the people to a system of bartering for everything they needed. For some time the Hume family lived on rye bread and suppone, generally known among families who have seen "rough" times as mush. The family's life was further aggravated by outbreaks of fever and ague. The terrain of their homestead was such that after each rain the water would not drain. Instead, it formed swamps which bred vast numbers of malarial mosquitos. As a result of the depression, fever and drought, the countryside about the Hume family was plagued by sicknesses, deaths, and bankruptcies during the year 1838. In the entire community only one man stayed well enough to work, and heroically he devoted most of his time drawing water and delivering it to his incapacitated neighbors.

The dreary years passed. As young Jim grew he began to rebel against his father's Puritan ways. The youth had no desire to spend his life on the farm fighting useless battles against droughts, rainy seasons, agues and fevers. His education had consisted of going to school during the winter months until he was fourteen plus an additional 24 weeks instruction in the Lagrange Collegiate Institute in Ontario. His sole interests at this time consisted of reading every available newspaper. His older brother, John, had become a lawyer but young Jim was too restive for "any such white collar occupation."

And then lightning erupted across Jim Hume's horizon! James Marshall's discovery at Sutter's Mill dominated the headlines of every newspaper and young Jim Hume devoured each word describing the happenings of the western regions. Secretly Jim and his brother John made many plans for treks to the gold country, but always the image of their disapproving father loomed across such plans, stilling them for the moment.

In 1850 the two brothers left the farm despite their father's wishes, organized a party of eight men and traveled to Chicago where they bought guns, camp equipment and other things needed for the trek west.

Eventually they reached Kanesville, later to be known as Council Bluffs. There they laid over for a short while to give the spring grass a chance to grow so that they would have feed for their horses and mules while enroute to the goldfields.

Slightly over three months later Jim and John Hume and their party (now numbering four) reached California. Selling their "worn-out" horses and mules for $140, they headed for the middle fork of the American River. When they reached their destination they spent $20 for a used shovel, then bought a rocker for $10. At last they were miners!

The Hume brothers knew nothing about mining, but neither did most of the others who had invaded the motherlode country. Wisely the brothers kept their mouths shut and watched the few real miners. And, oddly enough, after a period of hard work they weighed their dust and were surprised to find that they had amassed over a thousand dollars worth of the precious metal! They split the money with their two partners then dissolved the partnership.

The Hume brothers had decided to try their hands as merchants. Flour was selling $30 per hundredweight, potatoes and onions 40¢ per pound or higher and most everything else was priced accordingly. Finding a small building, the brothers operated a store for a short while and, despite the excessively high freight charges, netted 100% on their investment. By that time they had both decided they were not "cut out" to be merchants but were determined to stick with the store as long as their prosperity continued.

Eventually John Hume took up the practice of law in the gold country while Jim worked claim after claim. To "keep the vittles on the table" and a roof over his head, he drifted in and out of various jobs, eventually serving as a deputy sheriff in El Dorado County. Shortly afterwards he was appointed deputy tax collector in the little mining town of Placerville where his duties consisted of collecting the highly controversial Foreign Miner's License Tax. His remuneration in that job was 15% of the taxes he managed to collect. Proving capable, he was then given the job of dogcatching! He was teased unmercifully through the years by friends, foes, and even the newspapers about his dogcatching activities. But he did such a good job that finally the pendulum of public favor began to swing to his side. Newspapers began to praise him for the way he maintained the town's sidewalks, cleaned up the gutters, and kept the rabies scares and stray dogs under control.

Hume's life was filled with his duties from morning to night, a fact which created no hardship for him due to the early work habits learned from his father. Eventually he became town marshal of Placerville, handling routine cases of drunkenness, loitering and other minor violations while the sheriff's office took care of the murders, holdups, and more serious crimes. Hume solved one case where a merchant had been robbed of $20 cash, some quicksilver and a large supply of tea. Since there had been so much tea stolen Hume turned his attention to the Chinese criminal element, knowing that they were great tea drinkers and eventually captured six Oriental thieves who had plagued the community for some time. His success in this venture led to the local papers praising him for his ability. That article proved to be the first of many in the next few years.

Hume's success in a number of small cases brought him to the attention of Sheriff William H. Rogers who appointed him under-sheriff of Placerville, March 4, 1864. From tax collecting to dogcatching, and finally to the office of under-sheriff! Slowly but surely Hume was finding himself, further developing his powers of deduction and uncanny sense of what a criminal could be expected to do.

At 10 P.M., June 30, 1864, destiny provided the trigger which served to catapult Jim Hume into prominence! Two of Louis McLane's Pioneer Stage Company coaches were held up between Lake Bigler (now Tahoe) and Placerville. Seven outlaws, claiming to be a contingent of the Confederate Army, relieved the two coaches of coin and bullion originally estimated to be from $5,000 to as much as $40,000. Hume was out of the county at the time and his superior, Sheriff Rogers, rode out with a posse. Later Rogers split his group so as to cover more territory. Ironically the three men he sent to cover a local crossroads stumbled upon the holdup men who were hiding in a local hotel.

One of the three men slipped away to find the sheriff and his posse while the other two stayed to keep an eye on the bandits. But the two lawmen left behind became involved in a deadly shootout with the outlaws, resulting in the death of deputy Joseph Staples (one of Hume's closest friends) and the wounding of the other deputy and some of the outlaws.

Hume returned to Placerville as soon as possible after hearing of the trouble. For the next several days he and his men tracked the so-called Confederate raiders over several counties. Losing the trail, they were forced to return empty-handed. But Hume did not give up. During the next few weeks he questioned Tom Poole, one of the outlaws who had been wounded and captured during the shootout, and eventually broke the man down. Poole's confession resulted in Hume obtaining all the names of the men involved in the holdup.

Armed with this information Hume searched the countryside. And on August 1st, 1864, with only one officer at his side, crashed a meeting and arrested nine outlaws who had been involved in the robbery of the two stages. Although the outlaws had patterned themselves after Quantrell's Bloody Kansas Raiders and had vowed to fight to the death, they gave Hume and his deputy no trouble, surrendering meekly.

As a result of Hume's dogged pursuit and logic all of the stolen bullion was recovered and the outlaws arrested and brought to justice.

During the years Hume's reputation grew. In his life as a lawman he was successful in every way but one. He preferred to let his deeds speak for him rather than to "play politics." As a result of his frankness, plain talk, and refusal to "play the game," he was defeated when he ran for office. (Most authorities agreed that Hume was beaten due to the fact that he ran as a Democrat, and in that particular election the governor and all of the other candidates who ran as Democrats were soundly trounced.) One of the local newspapers summed the situation up in these words: "Personal spite and soreheaded disaffection in our ranks have defeated one of the best and most deserving officers this, or any other, county has ever had in its service."

The citizenry had a farewell party for Hume and presented him with a gold watch and chain as a token of their esteem. But Hume was stunned as a result of his political drubbing and perhaps the debacle greatly influenced him to take the offer of Lloyd Tevis and John Valentine shortly thereafter to head up Wells Fargo's detective force.

During his many years with Wells Fargo, Hume was never without a case to work on. It was a rough country, filled with rough men who had gambled on finding their fortunes in the gold country. And too often their failure to wrest a bonanza in the mines caused them to try to wrest it from the nearest Wells Fargo stage. In Neill C. Wilson's book, *Treasure Express,* is a highly informative table which shows the box score of the running battle between Wells Fargo and the stage robbers as of 1884:

Number of stage robberies	313
Attempted stage robberies	34
Burglaries	23
Train robberies	4
Attempted train robberies	4
Number of Wells Fargo guards killed	2
Number of Wells Fargo guards wounded	6
Number of stage drivers killed	4
Number of stage drivers wounded	4

Number of stage robbers killed 16
Number of stage robbers hanged by citizens 7
Number of horses killed 7
Number of horses stolen from teams 14
Convictions 240
Treasure stolen
   (promptly made good to customers) . .$415,312.50
Rewards paid 73,451.00
Prosecutions and incidental expenses ... 90,079.00
Salaries of guards and special officers .. 326,417.00
Total cost to Wells Fargo due to highwaymen
   operating against 8 trains and 347 stages,
   during 14 years $905,259.50

The fourteen years had cost Wells Fargo great sums but the company's vigilance had established a record that is regarded with awe when one considers the vast number of bandits and outlaws who rode the territory in search of gold at any price!

Hume was continuously studying the latest developments in criminology and in one case initiated the use of ballistics to secure convictions.

Early one Saturday morning in September of 1878, the Yreka-Redding stage was stopped on Scott Mountain. Three bandits, one wearing a typical Black Bart flour-sack, stepped from the shadows with guns levelled and demanded the stage's strongbox. Suddenly the Wells Fargo guard, John Reynolds, triggered his shotgun, driving the hooded figure backward into the ditch. Frantically the driver whipped his teams into a run but shots from behind struck the near wheel horse, killing it instantly.

And then the driver, Charles Williams, walked back, weapon in hand, and stood guard in the middle of the road while John Reynolds and the stage's only male passenger worked to strip the harness from the dead horse and rearrange the team to pull the stage on to its destination. For twenty minutes Williams stood there, a deliberate target daring the bandits to strike again.

Wells Fargo was notified and, as usual, Hume was soon enroute for the area. Meanwhile the local authorities arrived and identified the hooded figure found dead in the ditch as a shoemaker from Copper City.

The two bandits that escaped were captured the following day, after they had spent the night drowning their sorrow at the loss of their leader and the loot from the attempted robbery. Their reluctant host had managed to slip away during the night and notify the law.

Jim Hume, sensing the need for additional evidence, took some buckshot pellets from the dead horse and compared them with that found on the suspects. The buckshot was a rare, special type and Hume's ballistics work led to the conviction of the two robbers. According to all available records this was the first time that particular test had ever been used, another tribute to the keen mind of Wells Fargo's Chief of Detectives!

In 1881 Hume was called to Arizona to work on some

cases. After having visited Tombstone he described the town as follows:

> Six thousand population. Five thousand are bad. One thousand of these are known outlaws.

One of Hume's employees in Tombstone was Wyatt Earp. That worthy gentleman had first entered Wells Fargo's services in 1877 when he rode as shotgun guard from Deadwood City to Cheyenne, earning $50 and free passage. It had been a shrewd investment for Wells Fargo who had more than $200,000 in gold riding that particular stage. To further safeguard the shipment the canny Wells Fargo agent posted a sign advertising the run and stating, "Wyatt Earp of Dodge City, Kansas, riding shotgun."

In 1880 Hume reinstated Wyatt on Wells Fargo's payroll at Tombstone, hoping to curb the holdups of their stages by a variety of desperadoes including, notably, "Old Man Clanton" and his lawless gang. For a while Wyatt rode as special guard on the Tucson-Tombstone run and eventually (according to some authorities) his doing so may have been one of the factors that built up to the famous gunfight at the O.K. Corral.

Hume had a special axe to grind with the Clanton Gang. On January 9, 1882, *The Tombstone Epitaph* ran a column with the following subheadlines:

> SANDY BOB'S UP STAGE STOPPED LAST NIGHT. THE ROBBER'S REAP A LIGHT HARVEST. WELLS, FARGO'S CHIEF DETECTIVE STOOD UP WITH THE REST.

Hume had been on the Benson Stage's night run to Tombstone. Knowing that the stage carried no gold or other valuables and having had a very tiresome day he dozed off. Suddenly he was awakened. The stage was being held up by two men whom he recognized as Curley

Bill Brocius and Pony Deal. One of the men had stuck the business end of a sawed-off shotgun through the coach's window and demanded the passenger's valuables. Warily Hume considered the situation. It was obvious to him that if he offered any resistance the deadly shotgun would cut him and the other passenger's to pieces. Slowly he raised his hands. Laughing, the bandits took three revolvers and $75 from him. After that embarrassing episode Hume declared war upon the banditry of the "town too tough to die."

One of the most unusual of Hume's cases started shortly before dawn, October 11, 1894 when two bandits robbed the Overland Express two miles outside Sacramento. Under their orders of do-or-die the engineer unhitched his cab and moved it away from the train. Then the two outlaws got the drop on the express car messenger and stole $51,000 in gold. After forcing the train to move on, the two men faded into the night.

Hume investigated the train robbery but the gold and the two bandits were not to be found. He turned the problem over in his mind. How had the two men managed to get away with 200 pounds of gold bullion? While he was working on the mystery two men held up a train at Redding, California. During that holdup the sheriff of Tahama County was aboard. While trying to prevent the robbery of the passengers, he was shot and killed by one of the robbers. Suddenly the angry passengers attacked the killer. A shot rang out and he was dead. In the excitement the other bandit had gotten his horse and made his getaway.

Quickly Hume was on the scene. After a careful examination he mounted a horse and rode off alone on the outlaw's trail. Three days later Hume returned, the body of the bandit tied across his horse. The fugitive, known as Jack Brady, had forced Hume to shoot him when he resisted arrest. Dying, the man had confessed to the holdup attempt of the Redding train, and the earlier robbery of the train at Sacramento. Unable to move the 200 pounds of gold stolen in that robbery, he and his partner had dug a hole alongside the railroad track and buried it. When they returned to dig it up the gold was gone.

Temporarily stymied and with no clues whatsoever, Hume finally unraveled the mystery. He learned that a tramp had been sleeping alongside the track as the robbery was committed. Awakened by the noise, the hobo, later identified as Karl Heerman, born in Hamburg, Germany, had watched while the two outlaws buried the gold. When they left he hurriedly dug up the gold and buried it in a different location. Later, after the authorities had investigated and left the scene of the crime, he had dug up the gold and kept it for himself. Shortly afterwards he had gone on a long journey to New York City where he had spent $11,000 on wine, women, and song. Due to Hume's shrewd detective work the tramp was arrested, convicted, and served a sentence in Folsom Prison for his crime.

Today James Hume is regarded by many authorities as one of the most clever detectives of all time. The modern day lawman has radio, television, telephones and other such scientific discoveries to aid him in his work; but Hume had only his wits and what few clues he could find to break his cases.

Gradually Hume developed a sixth sense about his investigations and the people he interviewed. And due to that sixth sense he solved many cases that had been "written off." Deduction, interrogation, intuition, and the art of finding "patterns" woven through his cases were the ingredients that made Jim Hume the great detective that he was. These facts are evident in a careful study of Hume's capture of Black Bart.

Invariably the witnesses who had been aboard the stages Black Bart had robbed described the outlaw as "courteous, possessed of a deep, pleasant voice, tall, and definitely a young man." Hume released handbills and flyers bearing the above description, but he had long ago learned how confused witnesses could be when looking down a gun barrel. Patiently he traveled through the countryside around each of the holdup areas, asking questions and looking for clues. And at last the patterns he was seeking began to emerge.

At many of the holdup areas a kindly stranger had been seen, *always just before a holdup was committed!* And all had agreed that the stranger was very courteous and possessed of a deep voice. But there the similarity in the stranger's description and that of Black Bart ended. This stranger was only average height (although all agreed he stood very erect) and was definitely an older man. He wore a small white goatee and two of his front teeth were missing.

Hume was excited. Why would the stranger have been in the different localities just before a holdup if he was not the bandit? Carefully the detective studied the facts. He understood the discrepancy concerning the suspect's height, knowing that any average-sized man who stands erect looks ten foot tall to a witness staring down the barrel of his shotgun!

By using logic Hume also reasoned why witnesses said Black Bart was a young man. Since the outlaw always made his escape from the scene of his holdup on foot, traveling very fast through wild and mountainous terrain, Hume reasoned it only natural for witnesses to think him a young man. Generally speaking it was inconceivable that an older man could accomplish such a feat!

By such thought processes Hume uncovered another revealing fact. Each time Black Bart made a pretty good haul he faded away, not to be heard of again for some time. But when the loot had been small he had always struck again within the next day or so. Once again Hume had found his pattern! It led him to believe that the outlaw was an older man who lived in some nearby town or city, who only robbed a stage when his money was low. Also that the man lived modestly and laid low between each of his holdups. How accurate Hume's deductions had been became evident with Black Bart's capture.

Jim Hume possessed another quality that helped him break many of his cases. Always a kind, friendly man who liked people, he could talk to criminals and treat them humanly. His warmth and sincerity impressed them and led them to trust him, often resulting in a confession. Tough on wrongdoers while he was tracking them down, if he believed they still had some basic goodness inside them, he would often go to bat for them, pleading with the court for consideration, or even lighter sentences in some cases!

James B. Hume was a bachelor until he was 59. Then, on April 28, 1884, he married Miss Lida Munson, a lovely, spirited woman whom he had courted for several years.

During his last years Hume and his wife lived in Oakland, California, where he took special pride in his rose garden and other simple pleasures such as his favorite cheeses and special wines with his dinner. A simple man in his wants and tastes, he stayed on his job with Wells Fargo until he lost his final battle with sickness on May 18, 1904.

CHAPTER
VIII

FROM
THE PONY EXPRESS
TO
THE "IRON HORSE"

It was May the 9th, 1860 . . .

Pony Bob Haslam ran to the door of the crude log-cabin as his keen ears picked up the sound he had been awaiting. He bolted from the doorway, heading for the nearby hitching rack where his pony stood, munching oats from the nosebag. Quickly he removed the bag, grabbed the bridle hanging from the saddle horn, and "bitted" the animal.

Behind him the hoofbeats grew louder as the horse and rider drew near. Pony Bob stooped and tightened the cinch, then automatically checked the tie-down on the .45 Colt nestled on his hip. He drew a deep breath. He was ready.

Suddenly the rider from the west was clattering across the open clearing, a hundred yards away. Pony Bob Haslam stepped up into leather, left hands on the reins, right outstretched, waiting for the slap of the mochilla.

Then the mochila was in his hand, he was leaning forward, feeling the eagerness in his mount as they thundered down the trail. A few moments later they were pounding on the path bordering Lake Tahoe's bank, and soon out of sight as they climbed into the mountains and headed for Buckland's Station, seventy-five Paiute-infested miles to the east!

William H. Russell had ramrodded the project through in 65 days after getting the approval of his partners, Alexander Majors and William B. Waddell. It had been a mammoth undertaking, requiring approximately 119 stations to cover the 1,966 miles from St. Joseph, Missouri to Sacramento, California. 500 of the finest ponies available had been bought and distributed over the route, 200 station agents and various other workers had been hired to get the stations in order and to keep them going, and 80 brave young riders had been selected from among the many thousands who had read the Pony Express advertisement:

> Wanted—young, skinny, wiry fellows, not over 18.
> Must be expert riders, willing to risk death daily.
> Orphans preferred. Wages $25 a week . . .

Each man had a run of from about 75 to 100 miles. At one end of their route was their home station; there they lived, slept and ate between runs. Most of the route was laid out so that riders would have a fresh horse every 10 to 15 miles. However, in an emergency, the riders had to make out with their old mount when horses had been stolen or strayed away.

Pony Bob prepared himself as he rode into the station for a fresh mount. As he raced through the shadows he lifted the mochila over the saddle horn. He slowed his pony slightly, then was off its back and running, never breaking stride as he raced to his fresh mount. Quickly he seated the mochila, grabbed the horn as the mustang broke into a run, and pushed off with his feet. Then he was in the saddle and out of that station's clearing—next stop Reed's Station!

But there he was doomed to disappointment. There was no horse standing ready as he rode in. Breathlessly, the excited station agent told him that all of his stock had been appropriated by men from Virginia City; to be used in the forthcoming battle with the Indians. Bob Haslam shook his head warily.

Fifteen sweat-soaked miles later, the determined little pony raced into the hard-packed front yard of Buckland's Station. Once again Pony Bob Haslam was due for a surprise! His relief, Johnny Richardson, was not in the saddle, ready to ride. Instead, he was standing on the station porch, shaking his head negatively as he listened to W.C. Marley, the station agent.

Ten minutes later Pony Bob Haslam was mounted on a fresh pony, heading for the station at Sink of the Carson, thirty-five miles to the east. Johnny Richardson had refused to make his scheduled ride; the Indians were out and killing!

He arrived at the Sinks of the Carson without incident, then rode on for Sand Springs. He fought to stay awake in the saddle, watching his pony's ears, the best barometer should there be any Indians in the area. At last he made Cold Springs; only thirty miles more to Smith's Creek and a bed! A numbing weariness was flooding his body as he rode the last few miles. Then he was riding in and tossing the mochila to J.G. Kelley. He stumbled across the yard and disappeared in the shedroom built on the side of the main building. Pitching forward on the bed, he was asleep at once, oblivious to the world about him. He had ridden 190 miles during the past several hours, stopping only to change mounts and eat. His ride would be acclaimed as the greatest ride of all Pony Express men; but he was not yet through!

Nine hours later, he was in the saddle once more, retracing his journey, heading west to Friday's Station.

He rode in to Cold Springs to find gray smoke rising from the ashes of its buildings. A war party had run off the station's horses and killed John Williams, the agent. Haslam watched the skyline as he watered his pony. Anything could happen now!

Warily he raced toward his next stop at Sand Springs. Instead of riding on through as he would usually have done, he stopped and told the agent of the massacre at Cold Springs. Knowing the man would have no chance at all against a war party, Haslam suggested that agent ride with him to the Sink of the Carson Station. Regretfully the man did so. It proved a wise decision. The Sand Springs Station was attacked early the next morning!

When Haslam and the agent arrived at the Sink of the Carson, they found the agent and his stockhandler fortified with fifteen survivors of the Battle of Pyramid Lake. About 50 war-painted Indians had been in the area, estimating the station's strength and vulnerability. Now the survivors were armed and ready, expecting an attack at any moment. Haslam rested for about an hour, then rode on to Buckland's Station, arriving there only 3½ hours behind schedule!

W.C. Marley was tickled pink to see the nervy young rider again. When he learned of all that Haslam had been through, he gave him $100 as a bonus for making his daring ride instead of $50 as he had originally planned. He insisted that Haslam stay and rest for a while, but the hardy Pony Express rider was too excited and couldn't let down. An hour and a half later he was back in the saddle once more. He rode his usual route back to Friday's Station with no further trouble.

Despite the lack of fresh horses, danger from bloodthirsty Indians, and their burning of stations and murder of the agent, John Williams, the daring Pony Bob Haslam had ridden 380 miles in 36 hours, and was just a few hours behind schedule. His ride was destined to carve his name

As had generally been known from the beginning, the Pony Express could not help but be a money-losing proposition. But since Russell, Majors & Waddell's company was already on the verge of bankruptcy, they had plunged ahead with the Pony Express project, hoping that such a dynamic undertaking would gain the public's fancy and win them a lucrative contract to carry the U.S. Mail daily from the Missouri River to California. They were encouraged in the venture by Senator Gwin of California, who pledged them his support, and assured Russell that such a gamble was necessary if their company desired the mail contract. But despite all their efforts and hopes, the mail contract did not materialize.

In the last seven months of the 18-month Pony Express, Wells Fargo's role in it was a large and crucial one. It was partly direct and partly indirect through the control Wells Fargo by then was exercising over the affairs of the Overland Mail Company. The March 1861 government contract for U.S. Mail by both stagecoach and Pony Express on the central route went, not to Russell, Majors & Waddell who by then were practically flat broke, but to the Overland Mail Company with its powerful backing by Wells Fargo. Russell, Majors & Waddell continued to operate the part of the Pony Express line east of Salt Lake City, but did so as subcontractor to the Overland Mail Company. Until July 1, when the Overland Mail Company could get its stock and equipment up from the southern route to the central route, Wells Fargo took charge of the entire section of the Pony Express line west of Salt Lake City. After July 1, Wells Fargo operated the leg of the official Pony line over the Sierra between Placerville and Carson City and, as an accommodation to San Franciscans, ran a "private" Pony Express between San Francisco and Placerville to connect with its regular pony at the latter point.*

The completion of the transcontinental telegraph in the latter part of 1861 was the last straw for the Pony. Horseflesh couldn't outrun the lightning wire. It was a gallant venture, however, that, during its short life served well the increasingly pressing need for speedy communication between California and the East. The Pony Express made

---

*This paragraph, and much information scattered throughout this book, was furnished by the Wells Fargo Bank History Room.

308 runs each way, logging a total of 616,000 miles. It had delivered 34,753 pieces of mail, and had lost only one mochila. Approximately two-thirds of the letters had been sent by Californians; had the other states done as much, it might have been a different story.

Exactly nine years to the day after Pony Bob started his epic ride, people started converging at Promontory Point, Utah.

It was early morning, May 10th, 1869, when the porter knocked softly on the train compartment door, as though fearful of waking its occupant.

For a moment there was silence. Then a man's voice rang out, a voice obviously used to authority, "Yes?" There was a slight pause, then, "Oh, all right, porter. I'm awake now." As the train employee moved down the narrow aisle, there was a slight rustling noise as the man inside crawled from his bed and started preparing for the day. He yawned, stretched, and reached for his pocket watch. He thumbed open its golden lid and stared down at the dial, 5:32 A.M. Good, he had time to get some breakfast and to compose his thoughts before the rest of the delegation were up and about.

Mr. Judah had done a lot of the early groundwork. Too bad that he couldn't be here this day. He could still see Judah at that meeting way back in September of '59. Judah had impressed them with his ambition and plans for the project; as a result they had elected him their delegate to lobby in Congress, hoping to gain approval of the Pacific Railways Act.

In 1860 Judah had approached Collis Huntington, Charley Crocker and Mark Hopkins, asking them to invest in the Central Pacific. It had been such a good idea that they had agreed; also had underwritten Judah's expenses incurred while finding the best train route through the Sierras. Of course, Leland Stanford recalled, his being elected the first Republican Governor of California had served to expedite the ambitious project.

In 1862 Congress had finally passed the bill and Abe

Lincoln had signed it, thereby granting the Union Pacific a charter to build a railroad from Omaha to California. The government had agreed to loan the company $16,000 for every mile of track built over plains, $32,000 for each mile along the mesas and plateaus, and $48,000 per mile built through the mountains. In addition, Union Pacific was to receive free rightaways, free use of minerals and timber in the public lands, and a grant of 20 sections of government land for every mile of track that was built!

The Governor's corporation, the Central Pacific, had been granted the same terms and conditions, and had contracted to build east from California to meet the Union Pacific.

Those had been wild, turbulent years.

The land was a wilderness: Indians, deserts, bad weather, the almost impossible, impassable Sierras. Why, it had taken every bit of two years just to dig that tunnel through the granite ridge just above Donner Lake! The boys had called it 1,659 feet of Hell!

And the labor situation—where do you suddenly get 15,000 workmen who are ready to drop everything to build you a railroad?

Charley Crocker had told the story so many times that the governor knew it by heart. Originally Crocker had a deal going to use Mexican labor. But he'd got a letter at home one day, advising him that the deal had fallen through. He had been pretty well shook up, old Charley had, 'cause time was of the essence. He was setting there, scratching his head and worrying, when his Chinese man-servant, Ah Ling, brought him in some fresh coffee. Charley stared, thinking how hard Ah Ling worked, how loyal he had been, and so forth. Well, the next day he had had his foreman to hire 50 Chinese at Sacramento and send them to the end of track, hoping they might work out. It had been the greatest surprise of all. Those Chinese had appreciated their new job so much that they went all out. Almost immediately, Charley had hired two thousand more. It had been a great break for everybody concerned.

Supposedly, there had only been three Chinese in California in the year 1848. But with the gold strike and other things happening, their number had grown to nearly 70,000 by 1869. Greatly resented by the white miners, they had not been allowed to mine and have claims. So when cheap labor was needed to build road beds and lay track, the Orientals were ready.

Gradually the Chinese had figured in the great competition between the Union Pacific and the Central Pacific. Former Generals, Grenville Dodge and Jack Casement, had been ramrodding the Union Pacific, and one day "General Jack" had bragged to the newspapers that his "Irish Terriers" had laid 7½ miles of track in one day. When Charley Crocker heard, he had reporters brought in to watch as his Chinese workers set out to break the record. And they did, by laying over 10 miles of track in one day! Yessir, the Chinese had done well . . .

It was exactly 1,085.8 miles from the last tie at Promontory Point to Omaha, and 690 miles to Sacramento. Now, to symbolize their cooperation, engine No. 119 of the Union Pacific, and the engine, Jupiter, of the Central Pacific, moved up until they were only about thirty feet apart. At last Governor Leland Stanford and Thomas C. Durant took their places, one on each side of the rails. Then each drove a golden spike into the laurelwood tie. It was now official, at last the country had its transcontinental railroad!

The transcontinental railroad historically brought an end to the romantic era of stagecoach travel. However, it marked only a way station in the overall growth of Wells Fargo which saw many significant changes before 1869, and would see many more thereafter:

In 1860, after deposition of Butterfield from the presidency of Overland Mail Company, Wells Fargo assumed and thereafter exercised a controlling hand in the affairs of that company.

In 1863, its stages had made it possible for the company to haul $20,000,000 out of Virginia City.

In 1864, Wells Fargo bought the splendidly equipped and heavily traveled Pioneer Stage Line from Louis McLane and his brother Charles, who had acquired this line over the Sierra in 1860. Louis McLane since the mid-1850s had been Wells Fargo's general manager for California, and his line had been heavily employed by Wells Fargo for the transportation of its mail, express, and treasure shipments.

In 1866, Wells Fargo engineered a gigantic consolidation in which its express, banking, and stagecoach businesses were combined with the Overland Mail Company, Ben Holladay's Overland Mail and Express Company, and with the already-wholly owned Pioneer Stage line, together with certain express lines west of the Mississippi of the American and United States Express Companies. This consolidation was effected under Colorado charter and with it Wells Fargo & Company under its new president, Louis McLane, became "Sole Proprietor of the Great Overland Mail Route." Ben Holladay was paid off largely in cash and left the scene to pursue other interests in Portland, Oregon.

In 1867, Wells Fargo ordered a total of 40 new Concords from Abbott & Downing—30 at one time—to better serve their passengers and express customers.

In 1869, Wells Fargo closed down stage operations other than acting as feeder lines for the railroads; it sold its Salt Lake City-Uintah stage line to Gilmer & Salisbury, and its Argenta-Austin line to J.P. Cope & Co. From that day forward, well aware that the stage business was in a decline, Wells Fargo concentrated its energies on the expansion of its banking and express operations.

In 1872, Lloyd Tevis became president of Wells Fargo. He secured express privileges for his company with the Southern Pacific Railroad and the Santa Fe Railroad.

In 1876, Wells Fargo's express and banking departments, which always had been operated and accounted for separately, were for the first time housed in separate buildings in San Francisco.

In 1908, the last holdup of a Wells Fargo stage was accomplished when "bad guys" stole the box of the Rawhide-Manhattan Concord. The outlaws were chased by lawmen riding in touring cars and sports roadsters.

In 1952, having made continuous adjustments to the world about it, Wells Fargo celebrated its 100th year in business.

In 1960, Wells Fargo Bank merged with American Trust Company, in order to better provide the banking size and facilities necessitated by the rapid economic and population growth in California.

In 1975, Wells Fargo Bank, National Association, proud of its heritage, is the eleventh largest bank in the United States and third largest in California. *Banking . . . with a tradition.*